My Hands
Were Clean

Tom Bradley

Second Edition

Unlikely Books

My Hands Were Clean

Second Edition

Copyright © 2010, 2016 Tom Bradley
Cover Art: "Open Mind" © 2013, 2016 Nick Patterson
Book Design Copyright © 2010, 2016 Unlikely Books

ISBN-13: 978-0-9907604-7-4
ISBN-10: 0-9907604-7-2

Thirteen Dollars

Unlikely Books
www.UnlikelyStories.org
New Orleans, Louisiana

Publisher's Preface
to the 2016 Edition

My Hands Were Clean was Tom Bradley's twentieth of his twenty-seven, or so, published books. It was initially published by us, here at Unlikely Books, in conjunction with the now-defunct small-press printer/direct mailer, Make It New Media, LLC. It was published in one volume with *Dr. Gonzo: A series of loosely related essays on equality, visibility, and modern mental health, or, How the Mental Health System Drove Me Crazy* by Dr. Deb Hoag. (Tom Bradley has a doctorate, too, but you don't want him touching your psyche directly.) Both books use loose memoirs as entrances to social commentary. Deb's book is about overcoming and treating mental illness in the context of a dysfunctional medical industry. Tom's book is about acid, orgies, and how Aleister Crowley and Mormonism go together smoothly like Christian teens with Satanic t-shirts.

When these two books were initially published, they were, in imitation of Henry Rollins' 2.13.61 Press, published as a flip-book. If you were holding *My Hands Were Clean* right-side up, then *Dr. Gonzo* would be the back of the book, upside-down. *Dr. Gonzo*'s back cover was *My Hands Were Clean*'s front cover, and vice versa. This 2016 Edition, being the full and unaltered text of the 2010 Edition of *My Hands Were Clean*, makes several references to *Dr. Gonzo* and the flip-book format.

Make It New Media was an attempt, by myself and a few other small-press activists, to put print-on-demand technology directly in the hands of small-press publishers. Whatever merits its business plan lacked or possessed, it had one thing going for it: we at Make It New Media knew how to turn pieces of paper upside-down. The large print-on-demand publishers, for whatever reason, have forbidden upside-down text to all of their clients. This is technologically ludicrous and professionally fuckfaced, but it is specifically unfortunate in this instance, because *My Hands Were Clean* is a book that should be upside-down at all times. Just take a moment with Nick Patterson's cover art. Rotate it slowly. Stop. Did you see that? Did you manage to find your way back to this paragraph, afterwards? Have the psychedelics not hit, yet? Take a minute. Oh, do you not have your own? Don't worry, there's some hidden inside this volume. Turn the book upside-down, then lick every page, individually. Be careful with your saliva—you're still going to want to read it, when you're done and the mood hits. I can't tell you which page has the acid and which page has the molly, but you're going to want to read the book twice, once on each hallucinogenic, and then a third time while straight. If you accidentally ruined the book by licking it, be sure to purchase another copy. If you're the sloppy-tongued sort, you might want to do that now, in advance. Ready? Good. Vamp to coda. Read the quotes and turn the page.

–Jonathan Penton

...my responsibility to the gods was to write as I was inspired; my responsibility to mankind was to publish what I wrote. But it ended there. As long as what I wrote was technically accessible to the public...my hands were clean.

–Aleister Crowley, *Autohagiography*

I was feeling pretty emotional by now, so I took a deep breath. I was about to say to him, "Have you read anything by Tom Bradley?"

–Kek W., "Interview with the Unknown Science Fiction Writer"

My Hands
Were Clean

I.

Let's play this cocksucker from vamp to coda.
                                    –Charles Mingus

At the authentically rustic Telestial Spaw [*sic*], we humble paid-under-the-table employees are gearing up for the evening shift: rolling up sleeves, squinching ring-shaped muscles, and so forth.

Yonder in the celestial vault, through the gathering gloom, certain scrawny stars are elbowing dowdy planets. I'm no expert, but if I squint my eyes, this conjunction, or whatever it's called, appears almost significant enough to warrant a special observation here below. The eating of some medium-strength acid might be in order.

And can you guess who just happens to be pinching, between left thumb and forefinger, a dandy blotter? It features a phosphorescent chartreuse goat with tangerine granny teats, rendered in surprising graphic detail for a consumer item so inexpensively mass-produced. You can even see exquisite areolae orbiting the gravitated nipples. That's quality craftsmanship. I am proud to have bought American.

Slipping a tiny piece of paper into one's mouth is an inconspicuous act, and can be encompassed under the guise of picking one's nose (acceptable behavior here at the Telestial Spaw, for employees as well as guests). The pinkie distracts attention by spelunking the nostril, just long enough for the corresponding thumb to prestidigitate between the lips and deposit the payload, which has been pre-inserted under the nail. Slick, literally, as snot.

But I've never felt fair abusing controlled substances in the Telestial Spaw Pioneer-Style Steam Buffet where I am enslaved. The Mormon diners flinch so guiltily over their tepid saucers of Sanka. After all, Our Heavenly Father's original proscription, as revealed to the Prophet-Seer-Revelator in *Doctrine and Covenants,* was not against caffeine per se, but hot drinks. This entire tourist trap is a whole-body hot drink. Hence the misspelt name. Who am I to compound the turpitude among the trenchers?

On the other hand, something tells me I must not wax entheogenic under the open sky this evening, not with one of those horoscopical thingies topside. It's the summer of my penultimate year in high school, and, being so endearingly young, I still lean toward the timorous end of the behavioral spectrum.

Judging from the furtive behavior of Mr. Glasscock, my boss, and his "senior employees" (read *plural wives plus sundry old acolyte-flunkies*), tonight's astrology must be inauspicious in some fucked way. The celebration of events from which wholesome people flinch is a characteristic of these quasi-Kabbalistic spermo-gnostic Tantric types, who make a point of savoring the End Times, or Latter Days, as they're known among the locals.

Being genetically fifty-percent "local" myself, I, too, am burdened by this tendency toward ritualism. I can't resist the innate urge to Eucharize, considering what strange spiritualities might be the neurochemical effect of the substance which my thankful head is about to receive. I need to collate the paper in my mouth with certain gyrations. And, in that context, it's always best to remember the exhortation of our Real Boss, the Big Mr. Glasscock in the Sky, who, long ago, opened his reverend mouth and taught the multitudes, saying—

When thou prayest, enter into thy closet.
And when thou hast shut the door,

pray to thy Father, which is in secret,
and thy Father which seeth in secret
shall reward thee openly.

So I need to take my act indoors. If not the chow hall, what is the obvious choice–because it is the only choice in this institution of exactly two structures, not counting subterranean steam and cream chambers and their locker room annexes? (The latter are beyond consideration; unlike Mr. Glasscock, I'd rather not be surrounded by naked, sweaty bodies at the delicate psychospiritual moment when that blotter goat succumbs to the enzymes in my saliva.)

Where's the best and only indoor place to perform the pre-evening-shift sacrament? Why, Shitland Pony Hell, of course. That's what we vulgar proles have nicknamed the Telestial Spaw Righteous Wrangler Riding Stable. It's home to a string of odd-toed ungulates whose wretched karma is to crack vertebrae under the anuses of city slickers from down in the valley. The tin-horn dudes among our clientele like to do a little pretend horseback riding before boiling their bodies in the fluid discharge of our salt and tar desert.

Yes, that's right: salt and tar. Plenty of sulphur and radium, too. My place of employment is damned deep in the sort of godforsaken wilderness about which the prophet Isaiah, hewn in twain by a wooden saw for his efforts, warned us all–

...where demons and monsters shall meet,
and the Hairy Ones shall cry out one to another!

At such an early stage in my half of this flip book, I'm unwilling to commit myself with regard to demons and monsters. But nowhere will you find greater numbers of Hairy Ones than in Shitland Pony Hell. It's out back behind the restaurant, tucked among the fumaroles, solfataras, mini-geysers, mud pots and other sorts of volcanic razzmatazz that have turned these few acres into something more than just another expanse of extreme occidental zilch. Yellowstone on Quaaludes.

The Telestial Spaw Righteous Wrangler Riding Stable's ass-end has been wedged and tacked against an arc of the largest geothermal formation. Shaped, colored and even textured exactly like the lid of a colossal human skull, dominating the otherwise featureless landscape for miles around, this half-buried gargantuan noggin is our trademark. In a similar way another skullish outcrop advertized Golgotha.

Our giant cranium is composed of a precipitate stone which geologists from the local land grant college have designated *travertine*. It's the very material Nero caused to be quarried in grotesque quantities when he felt the whim to corrupt Rome with a similar den of crowded, diseased, smelly social resort. Up from deep within oozes our colossal Spaw Gawd's hot spinal fluid, our saleable commodity, whose ostensible salubriousness has prompted four generations of entrepreneurs to chase away the Uncompahgre aboriginals and charge admission to everyone else.

The chartreuse blotter goat starts butting its tangerine titties against the ridges of my thumb print. My teen-boy salivary glands respond with hunger, and commence dragging me toward the riding stable, lower jaw first, like a prognathous gorilla. I must hurry, as the evening shift is about to commence. That mustn't happen without my head well on the way to fucked-uppedness.

Supposedly in the eighteen-sixties, or the nineteen-thirties, or some unimaginably antique epoch like that, our strange old stable was cobbled together from such cellulose as this life-loathing ecosystem allows. After nourishing the neighborhood Uncompahgres for 500 years with beautiful, fatty pine nuts, the precious few pinyon trees were "harvested," their timbers chopped to size, creosoted, and sandwiched Lincoln log-style with native juniper limbs. I suspect the early owner-proprietors in those frontier days were no less Tantric than the current Glassy Cock, if they so systematically denuded their homestead of juniper. My injun confidant assures me that particular conifer, when green, oozes an antiseptic and pesticidal resin which repels demons, monsters and Hairy Ones as effectively as bugs and bacteria.

The sole remaining relic indigene is Augie the Stable Master. Though a convert to the faith of Brigham Young, and despite having his chief traditional source of fat denied him, Augie the Uncompahgre has been deemed by Mr. Glasscock unfit to work near food, and has been enslaved as ostler instead, because his hands are browner than mine. He's my pal, and lets me slink among his swaybacked charges and do my bad head rituals in exchange for Winstons, which he esteems more highly than any derivative of ergot. Augie's people are staunch peyotists and don't trust any nostrum from which sand needn't be scraped.

This outbuilding was semi-countersunken into the hot volcanic side of our Golgotha as an economical and ecological means of preserving the livestock from the horrid sub-zero temperatures which our local mercury absolutely never sinks to. This misapplied architectural trope was a Northwestern Euro-atavism on the part of the Scandinavian converts whom the Mormons enticed across the Atlantic in the nineteenth century. The great blond beasts could never be reconciled with the fact that they'd allowed themselves to be duped into peopling a desert, and today the tiny pinto beasts must suffer for it. Their perpetual state of foamy perspiration, either being ridden or bound in a sauna, explains the ponies' etiolated condition. Augie the Stable Master, on the other hand, was bred to thrive under sweat lodge conditions.

If you stand back with him and me and survey this horsey hoosegow and the planetary pimple against which it stands, you might be inclined to suspect it serves an esoteric function beyond, or rather beneath, its obvious utility. What is the real reason for a structure to be so oddly suction-cupped against a bone-white convexity of weirdly warm travertine like a cork plugging a black hole?

If, for some hideously unimaginable reason, you were to waste as many evenings of your incarnation hanging around the Telestial Spaw as I do, you'd notice, on certain muggy dusks when the underlying vulcanism seems especially malignant, a shadowy procession filing into the Righteous Wrangler Riding Stable. This parade of mumblers and chanters will comprise far more individuals than there is room for, considering the ranks of sentient beings whose space they are invading. And they don't leave—unless it is to creep out into the light of some ostensible sick dawn which even juvenile I am too wise to linger and witness.

Augie the Uncompahgre will have ushered in the leader of this procession with greater obsequiousness than the more famous porter showed the thane of Fife. But, like his predecessor, our redskin pal gives the impression, even through the sulphurous steam, that he considers his job to resemble that of Hell's gatekeeper. You might be forgiven for wondering if this rickety old barn is the vestibule of Perdition's rumpus room.

Now hear why your narrator hovers near the entrance/exit of Shitland Pony Hell and rarely dares penetrate deeper. Triple digits of years ago splinter-Mormon pioneer hands gouged a semi-secret chamber in the back wall, and deep under the floor. The base of our Spaw Gawd's occipital bone was trepanned, right where the perforation of his vertebral canal would be, to tap nothing less than our squalid establishment's Talu Chakra (whose seed syllable is—you guessed it—*aum*). Soul-lethal suction is capped by a stout door of imported oak, bound by iron bands.

City slickers who delve too deeply among the dark pony stalls in search of a ride for the afternoon are further discouraged (as if more discouragement were needed, considering the racket that rises from within) by five words, burned an inch deep with red-hot pokers into the wood—

PRIVATE BATH
BY RESERVATION ONLY

It's a hell hole, this Private Bath, as literally as it can be. Satan's rank sweat rises up to sulfurate the place and make it unwholesome. This evening, thanks to astrology and so forth, the Private Bath's hot stalagmite innards will writhe with oldsters' floppy tits and lumpy buttocks, both male and female. Varicose veins will slither like livid worms in physiological nooks I never knew existed. The Limping Sage himself, when he ranted the apocalyptic passages of the *Vishnu Purana* so many millennia ago, cringed from predicting a Kali Yuga so creaky and offputting.

Up from the ground comes the dutifully depraved racket of my elders. No evening shift for them. There must, indeed, be something noxious cooking in our particular niggling solar clump. Even though it's early in the evening of a business day, as opposed to the inky deeps of a Sabbath midnight, the grownups are celebrating the dreaded *Mass of the Phoenix*. I mean, they're celebrating it to the burlesque extent their peaked-out physiques permit. To drown them out, the Isaiah in my head raises his voice again and continues to prophesy as follows:

> *There hath the Lamia lain down, and found rest for herself.*

Speaking of the latter personification of offputting sex, tonight's Kali avatar is the butt-nekkid fifth plural wife of Mr. Glassy Cock. It's her turn to play Priestess-Succubus-Noisy Pain in the Ass. She screeches the inspired scripture of the Wickedest Man in the World, author of this half of our flip book's affecting title. Crowley would pop a hernia laughing at her post-menopausal white slum Provo accent mush-mouthing his revelation. Reciting from a priceless original 1913 edition of *The Book of Lies* (how in Baphomet's name can such a bibliophile's wet dream be sopping secretions in a sweat lodge—in Utah, yet?), Mrs. Glasscock-Five rhymes *swear* and *prayer* with *spar*—

> *Behold this bleeding breast of mine*
> *Gashed with the sacramental sign.*
> *I stanch the blood, the wafer soaks,*
> *High Priestess moistened death invokes.*
> *This Bread I gorge, this Oath I sw'ar*
> *As I enflame myself with pra'r.*

Please remember this is my junior year in high school. You and the teen-boy I are being exposed to Mrs. Glasscock-Five's yowling in the dimly recollected epoch when such "transgressive" behaviors still retained a certain amount of inverted social cachet. This was before every piece of trailer crap who hadn't anything like the cerebral cortex required to encompass actual blasphemy went to orgies once or twice a week, before Wal Mart greeters and Big Mac flippers bared their unbleached anuses for group turd-sex, duly YouTubed, because it's "so-fisty-cay-tud."

They have no idea how sophisticated. Even at the height of the English Renaissance, such brave men as John Dee funked bonerism outright. Goetic lubriciousness drove crop-eared Kelley outdoors in fastidious horror of the Daughter of Fortitude's loose tongue. Tonight that tongue malodorizes the fifth wife of my boss, but drives nary a splinter-Mormon out of the Private Bath and into the stable with holy Augie and blameless me.

I have stopped and frozen just inside the entrance to Shitland Pony Hell, safely in from under the stars, yet too teeny-timorous to get any closer to that caterwauling sphincter. I've assumed the official apprentice hippy acid-dropping stance: feet spread, knees slightly bent, flaps of forehead flesh cinched with charlie-horse torsion. Augie the Uncompahgre squats nearby, commiserating over a tiny split hoof and chewing on a couple crispy Brigham Young tea shrub cones. He tries to make chit-chat, which betrays a surprising unawareness of the semi-sacred nature of what I am about to do. Solemn silence would be more appropriate, because the phosphorescent chartreuse goat with the tangerine Baphomet boobs is about to descend to my own Private Bath, to bleat and invoke in the microcosmic steam and cream chamber that is my stomach.

Augie says, "I don't like it when Mrs. Glasscock-Five's turn rolls around to be priestess. She gets too enthusiastic too soon. They have to put a grocery bag over her head when parading her through here, because she makes such ugly grimaces it stampedes the ponies."

"And here I thought only spaniels and bonobos recognized human facial expressions."

"Talk about getting the toes stepped on. Spoil my moccasins."

"They look more like wing tips."

"I like to look nice for the patrons."

I don't want to be rude. But it's not easy to banter with a softspoken Turtle Islander over the sounds of such a weird sister filtering through the tiny wads of manure and masticated alfalfa. Before houseling myself on the body and blood of Albert Hofmann, I need a moment of hushy-hush to get ready for my job of degrading, monotonous manual shit work.

Oh, by the way, you needn't take that penultimate word literally. Not all boring toil involves contact with impure substances, and not everyone suffering servitude in an eatery must pollute his person with food residue. Amp up the ambient pretension, and it's not just their gullets the patrons want glutted with unctuous, saccharine crap. Take a moment to think about eardrums as well, and you might begin to suspect a secondary form of Steam Buffet bondage.

Meanwhile, I must take one last un-LSD-addled moment of my own to focus on those means of production which are literally in the hands of this particular member of the working class.

"Listen up, you big ugly coarse, oafish, bristly cunts," I wordlessly tell my many thumbs. "You've got to articulate the fugato passage in the Mozart transcription with the utmost lucidity. Otherwise that beautiful bus girl with the flaring nostrils who lugs gigantic trays of authentic Mormon pioneer cuisine past your work station will cease ever-so-superciliously to feign interest in 'one day soon' accompanying you ten spastic louts to the Secret Sex Pot, where she might submit to finger-fucks from those of you who behave yourselves during the Allegretto."

The Secret Sex Pot is a place of nice fucking, not transgressive (or so I have been told). Quiet and subtle, it's tucked on the wilderness side of our trademark geothermal formation, a zone known only to us employees, a strangely plant-friendly nookie-nook where Mrs. Gaia Terra has obliged us by opening the way into a small spherical side vault, a place where she has spread her thighs to the nighttime, erupted some of her metabolic fluids, shed some of her damp heat, and vouchsafed us a globe of dark green among the treelessness. The obvious is encompassed there between shifts—or so, again, I have been told.

You will recall, in this half of our flip book's opening paragraph, the offhanded way in which I identified with manual laborers. Now see me express romantic interest in one of them, a squalidly declasse food service employee yet, a horny-handed daughter of pink-collar toil, a "beautiful bus girl with flaring nostrils" who strains muscles bigger than those of the fingers to the tune of some sort of music evidently produced by your sly old narrator—who really had you going, right?

When you hear me use phrases like *we mere unbenefitted workers-with-our-hands*, you might at first assume it's an attempt at disarming self-effacement on the part of an intelligentsia-type prick. If you'll consent to ignore the hygienic implications of my insistence on making a hot bath integral to my tryst with this member of the Great Unwashed, you might even detect some bone-deep biological Marxism. Do I class myself amongst capitalism's light infantry, the unskilled drudges of this declining Kali Yuga?

Well, before you even think about making a past participle of *skill* in my vicinity, you might want to wait till you hear my several thumbs render this ostensible Mozart transcription. The wait won't be as long as I'd like.

Suddenly, as I stand here with no instrument in sight, my not-so-joyful noise manifests out of thick air, shying the livestock and making even kind-hearted Augie wince. Shameful deformations of Haydn's younger pal–unmistakable as my own because so atrocious–slither up from the cackling midst of the granny group-grunt downstairs, osmosing through the travertine like carcinogenic mercury vapors.

How is this possible? Is there some bona-fide conjury being performed in the Telestial Spaw's Private Bath? Is Mr. Glasscock really the incarnation of Aleister Crowley his wives believe him to be? Has he necromanced his star employee's astral shell and put it to work?

If so, I resent it, and not just because I'm not on the cock and the blotter hasn't kicked in yet. If Venus and the bit-fingernail moon and Saturn and crap like that happen to be rattling around in perverse ways upstairs, there simply must be shenanigans behind this iron-banded oaken door. And, heavenly bodies delineating a precis of the here-and-below, the result will be no less gravitationally inevitable than embarrassing. But it's neither the bumps and grinds overhead nor the gerontological rut-grunts underfoot that chagrin.

If you listen closely (no easy task), you'll detect incongruities layered under the music. In the background can be heard, not the dribbly noises one would associate with a private bath, but the racket typical of the Telestial Spaw's Pioneer-Style Steam

Buffet during business hours. Somehow, Mr. Glasscock has managed to transplant into his satanic fane not only me, but the racket I must compete with professionally: the mumbles and belches of peckish patrons and the klunks of their flatware against the unsanitary yet quaint oaken trenchers upon which are presented the rustic deep Crisco-fried gristle of hanta-viral rodents snared in dry washes hereabouts.

The tape recorder is one curse of modern technology, unlike the Steinway grand, which Mozart's ghost must be grateful for never having had to contend with. My own crap, specifically the set I performed for yesterday's late afternoon Steam Brunch, has been magnetized to mylar and lugged like a vat of stringy gray vaseline into this evening's inverted cannibal orgy. I'm like Nixon, except I use an inanimate object to belch gross expletives better deleted–and not just eighteen and a half minutes' worth. The whole brunch set could use gapping.

Yes, that's your narrator's handiwork gagging and scraping through the Hell-portal and vibrating the pygmy pony poopoo under your heels, via the expedient of a battery-operated boom box or ghetto blaster, or whatever they are called this year. If Jack Parsons played Prokofiev when conjuring his Moon Child way out there in Pasadena land, Glasscock considers my "heavenly" music a fit accompaniment to his infernal behaviors. Sometimes, during work, when I'm not looking (which is to say, dozing off in the middle of one Andantino or another), the boss causes the beautiful bus girl with the flaring nostrils to sneak a microphone among the girlie mags on my music stand.

Those last two words are an instrumental hint. You may construe them to signify that my multiplicity of thumbs don't render Mozart transcriptions on one of those upright portable glockenspiel doodads which get strapped to the titties for a marching band. It would be difficult to tuck a mike unnoticed onto a music stand clamped three inches from the performer's nose, no matter how deep in REM he'd sunk. (You're wondering why I am being so coy about supplying specs for the tool of my trade. You'll cease wondering soon enough.)

An inverted Eucharist needs liturgical music, I suppose. But, even in the context of fisted menses and swilled semen-curds, these sounds are obscene–and not just due to poor analogue reproduction. Let's just say our quasi-Kabbalistic spermo-gnostic Tantric orgiast brethren have not chosen to play back the most satisfactory number in my repertoire.

Left-path liturgy, like right-path, lends itself to ornamentation. But why Mozart? More to the point, why my unconscionable butchery of Mozart? Why my sacrilegious insistence on transcribing him for an instrument he was known literally to bend over and fart at? And why the transcription whose fugato passage I try so hard to make palatable to the beautiful bus girl with the flaring nostrils?

As I tongue-plaster the acid blotter like a scurrilous handbill to the wall of my own built-in cavern of overindulgence, I wonder why these flirters with damnation insist on having me present during their creepy rites. Is my rendering of the old masters so egregious as to serve the purposes of Tantric types, whose mission in this terminal age is to transgress the natural gag reflex that ugly old lady clitorises should excite? Are my hands so dirty as to have turned the brightest angel of the late Eighteenth Century to aural excrement to be gobbled by coprophagous ear-holes?

Just as that question writhes into my head, along with the LSD's preliminary brain shudders, my redskin sidekick suddenly (more or less, to the extent that suddenness is available to cats so attuned to the planetary slouch) rises from his tribalistic hunker beside the horsies' murky water trough, and casts his Winston butt aside.

"You'll never guess," he says, "which significant personage is praying more fervently than anybody else in the Private Bath at this very moment."

As if on cue, a shriek, so piercing as to traumatize the roots of the teeth, drowns out my disgraceful bungling of a certain *acciaccatura* (or is it supposed to be an *appoggiatura*?).

"Mr. Glasscock's mom? I wonder what she looks like. Maybe she's manifested too translucent to tell through the billows of fatty smoke."

"Jimmy Page."

"Patti who?"

Augie re-whispers the name with reverence usually reserved for an alias of Beelzebub in this evil sink of splinter-Mormonism. It bears repetition one more time, this moniker, to make up three, just like a conjure-formula scrawled in menstrual blood on so many consecutive leaves of an abortionist's recipe book.

Suddenly a second shriek geysers through the ground, rendering even more unwholesome the air of this orthographically challenged noplace.

II.

By the rivers of Babylon, there we sat down, yea, we wept, when we remembered Zion. We hanged our harps upon the willows in the midst thereof.

—Psalm 137: 1-2

It was in unclouded consciousness that Mr. Glasscock caused the unwarranted *W* to be wiped like an idiot booger on the end of the second word of his business place's name. This he did on perverse purpose in order to win the allegiance of the sub-literate local clientele, hayseed Mormons all, who come for the grub. They leave the steam and cream chambers and the rides on spavined nags to the city slickers, who, in their turn, wouldn't be caught dead with a mouthload of the trenchered crap we sling at the Telestial Spaw Pioneer-Style Steam Buffet, nor an earload of the live Muzak with which I season it.

Our diners are the same sort of people who, in an act of corpo-rocratic solidarity, eat as though hell-bent on developing diabetes, and succeed more often than not. The hypertension is palpable in the air. My job description is to "provide the good Latter Day Saint brethren with pink slathery clouds of aural Pepto Bismol." The Glassy Cock actually snickered those words at me during my audition, revealing an incongruous vocabulary and, I suppose, wit.

My boss is obviously no hereditary Latter Day Saint. He converted to Mormonism for access to local business connections, even to the extent of purchasing himself election as neighborhood "bishop." The extra wives aren't exactly a drawback, now that the Abrahamic dispensation no longer obtains.

The Glassy Cock himself is a small, pale and pointy schismatic Mo-Mo, with colorless eyes. His voice is the merest of whispers, and he feigns to speak in that special suburban Mormon accent, mincing and obliging and soft, the tip of the tongue nipped with sufficiently nice precision on the sibilants, just enough to convince any susceptible male adults within earshot that he's trying to get them to seduce him cruelly, right there on the spot. Meanwhile, his gigantic-mouthed Primary Spouse–any number of junior Glasscocks' sperm-plus-egg-type conduit to this particular generated existence–will be rolling around in the vicinity, wearing the preoccupied face of the sanctioned multiple adulteress.

The Glassy Cock dresses himself in fetching leisure suits. And an integral, if incongruous, component of this Mormon's womanish graciousness, is an aura he exudes of infinite stinginess. Somehow, it was obvious to me from day one that he was going to be the type of boss who would cause his bus girls' and musician's tips to be pooled at the end of each shift, giving the house a substantial cut; the type of boss out of whom the oppressed workers should expect to have to wheedle, cajole and grovel every single fucking under-the-table paycheck.

Your narrator, whom we'll provisionally call Tom Bradley, had developed a whole set of theories about "these people." Tom Bradley, himself, was fifty-percent "these people," in much the same way that other cantankerous tunester, Richard Wagner, was fifty-percent Jewish–or so they say. But he nevertheless put forth his hideous, almost genocidal theories, tapping stores of psychic energy which seemed to come from somewhere mysterious. No polygamist-Satanist spawn, Tom was possessed of but a single mother; but that one was a doozy, who had to swallow enormous dosages of chemotherapeutical substances such as lithium (second cousin to travertine) to counteract her cerebral cortex's biochemical whims, and had spent a large part of her life behind soft pastel bars. So Tom deserved a bit of petulant self-indulgence, perhaps. Someone with such negative charisma could never be politically dangerous, anyway.

As vile a specimen as The Glassy Cock might have been, according to Tom's theories, he had nevertheless managed to retain a bevy of the most ingratiating older women outside of the original cast of *Hush, Hush, Sweet Charlotte*. Tom had heard it whispered that these ladies were not only The Glassy Cock's secret plural grandmothers, but his wives as well. You'd be better off not believing a word of that. It wouldn't be necessary to dig so deeply to recruit an army of ingratiating older women around these parts.

There is a whole species of rural Mormon female, theoretically speaking, who, even alone or at ease with her intimates, assumes an air of ever-so-sweet solicitude. In her manner is an absence of aggressiveness, discontent, sarcasm or critical intelligence. Judging from her facial expression when she thinks she's not being observed, I reckon she most assuredly, in her heart-of-hearts, operates in this Hildegarde-von-Bingenish way internally. She must even discourse in blamelessness to herself during moments of solitude, when she's alone in the desert, or taking a shit (do people like this in fact take shits?), or swilling fistfuls of semen while standing naked on her head in the Private Bath. Her nature is fey and ingenuous. To somebody like Tom, she seems mighty cloying, especially so soon after a boyhood presided over by his brilliant harpy of a mommy, who was such an opposite type that it's only Tom's presence on the planet that makes the proximity of her and semen, even for a moment, plausible.

The Glassy Cock, who affected the outwardly sweetness of these old creatures as a means of concealing his own quasi-Crowleyan turpitude, was sensitive enough to the symptoms of through-and-through goodness to have hand-picked as his minions and administrative assistants a half-dozen or so of the primest, most sublime specimens of this type. They, in their turn, had soaked themselves in that special old-lady perfume that smells like ballpoints and stamp pads, and had excited eternal loyalty among the bus girls, establishing the sort of camaraderie that can only occur in the tightly-knit "family" which is being nurtured, as it were, under the auspices of several beneficent mothers.

The many gentle grandmother-figures may, in the evenings, have served as horrendous extraordinary mistresses of the perverted Eucharist. They may have taken their clothes off and become those spotty billows of climacteric bloat which the Tantric initiate is pleased to embrace in order to suppress, which is to say transgress, the normal granny-gag reflex. But in their aboveground personas, the several dozen Mrs. Glasscocks had lent the Telestial Spaw the nearest semblance of stylishness attainable so close to the fumes of the Great Salt Lake. They had whipped our rustic resort into ship-shapedness, and transformed it into the kind of place where Robert Redford deigned to appear with his retinue on those gray days when he found his "Sundance Kid" ski resort in nearby Provo Canyon to be almost as insipid as himself.

One slow afternoon the diminutive movie star borrowed some high-rise cowboy boots from the stable, ventured up to the house musician and muttered, with little fanfare, "How you doin'?" And Tom Bradley replied, "Better than you." Upon which Redford skipped a beat, then, in a formal tone of voice, complimented Tom on his playing.

"Oh, thank you, Mr. Beatty!" Tom had gushed.

It must've been disorienting for this famous Hollywood personality to meet such a gargantuan man with such a severe case of "small man's syndrome," that preemptive feistiness normally observable only in tiny males who have been the victims of bullies all their lives. Why did Tom pounce on others more distinguished than himself with the typical talons of the short person? Who could've been the bully who bullied enormous Tom?

III.

Would you know if a people be well governed, if its manners be good or bad? Examine the music it produces.

—Confucius

Augie the Uncompahgre clears his throat and makes a certain mournful face that indicates he's about to raise his naturally irenic voice to White-Eyes levels of volume. The Stable Master wants to be heard over Mrs. Glasscock-Five's subterranean descants and the accompanying cassette-recorded me trying to whang and twang over my inattentively brunching audience.

"You don't believe me, do you?" he says.

Someone, either me or a pony, whinnies in response. I feel the need to clarify a bit.

"Of course I don't. A smart indigene like you, planning to spend the rest of his life slaving in a rube dump like this? Ever heard of quotas, affirmative action? You could thumb a semi into town and get tenure or a county commissionership or something."

"No, no. I mean—"

"How about we hash this over later? I must get my ten thumbs into that meditative state of calm pertness required to play any musical instrument well, except maybe the mouth organ."

"—you don't believe me when I tell you who belongs to that extra voice shrieking in the Private Bath. Or else you do, but you're just pretending not to know who he is, like when Butch Cassidy or whoever came around. I sympathize. I think you'd be afraid to shake with Jimmy Page. His pick-hand could squeeze this part-time gig right out of you. Then you'd have to stop scabbing."

"I'm too young to join the musician's union."

"You could be a Youth Member. Cheaper dues," replies Augie. Thoughtfully he toes certain vegetable materials which carpet Shitland Pony Hell.

With the exception of the unclassifiable greenery that makes the Secret Sex Pot sexy, the only plant life Glasscock has allowed to remain is the Brigham Young Tea Shrub famously peculiar to this desert. Augie spends his free time plucking the tiny cones from this magic plant and scattering them in and around the fodder trough. He even hand-feeds the droopier ponies as we talk. With the herbalistic wisdom of all native folk, Augie instinctively esteems these cones as a natural source of ephedrine, that favorite adulterant of MDMA, which is a brand-new street drug this year of my high school career. It's also a popular means for weight lifters to achieve the delightful effects of aortic aneurysm. The ponies (who are not really Shitland, or even Shetland, but just plain old galled and jaded quarter horses of inferior blood and malnourished growth patterns) are supposed to eat these crispy reproductive organs with their supper because, as Augie explains, "It makes them give good ride."

"Regular buckin' broncos," he remarks, chucking one of his charges under the spittle-stalagmited chin.

"I resent the implication that I am scabbing. His Necromantic Nibs, the Infernal Glassy Cock-666, would never pay scale, anyway. And, besides–"

Yet another shriek, which my ears are reluctant to find familiar, seeps up through the Shitland Pony shit and interrupts what I'm trying to say, which my brain, now starting to dissolve in its acid bath, forgets.

"Jimi who?" I mutter.

IV.

...music, I regret to say, affects me merely as an arbitrary succession of more or less irritating sounds.
—Vladimir Nabokov

Maybe you can forgive such unhipness in a performer whose musicianship is not so much classical as clinical. Young precocious Tom Bradley had already needed, way back in ninth grade, two whole years ago, to rebuild his hallucinogen- and amphetamine-devastated nervous system through vigo-rous neural discipline, to lift himself out of the condition quaintly known in those days as "burnt-outedness," to restore himself to the former alertness and sharpness with which he had graced the universe in his latency period. He needed to re-route the relays of his deep-fried axons and dendrites on bridges of their own scar tissue, to circumvent, or even flush out, the opaque matter deposited in his early teen-aged brain's fatty synaptic clefts by years of THC, LSD, MDA, PCP, DMT, SPT and a whole alphabet of other powdered idiocies.

Who had time to keep pace with the latest passers-by in the Hit Parade? Likewise, Tom was literarily unhep, poorly versed in the writers of the time, such as What's-his-Jewish-Whoozit who did that thing featuring a watered-down version of Crowley's Ape of Thoth, about the "disorder in which strongly-felt ethical and altruistic *blah-blahs* are perpetually warring with extreme sexual *yaw-w-w-wns*, often of a perverse *sn-n-n-n-nores*." The words of Tennyson, instead, were ringing in poor Tom's already permanently tinnitus-cursed ear-holes, as follows:

> *I held it truth, with him who sings*
> *To one clear harp in divers tones,*

> *That men may rise on stepping-stones*
> *Of their dead selves to higher things.*

The dead self-stones were already eroding to grit between the walls of the lad's skull. It was creepy to assume that the entity Tom, he, was nothing but some vulnerable glops sloshing in a calcium box. Such antivitalism grated on a spirituality swollen as his. But still the tall teenager forced himself to proceed from just that assumption. And he whipped himself back into shape with the cat-o'-nine tails known as Mozart, transcribed and executed on a certain no-frills, stripped-down, strictly manual version of a keyboard instrument which will, for now, continue to remain nameless.

An unwieldy contrivance of birch, brass and catgut waited each afternoon and evening in Mr. Glasscock's chow hall to be shoved like a dildo between Tom's thighs. It had been his disease for twenty-four months. The infection had set in when he was only fourteen, a mere cherub: six-eight and three quarters, two hundred and ninety-six pounds.

He'd been trying his best to convalesce from the drug-drenched first/last love of his life with one Malka Knopfdrucker, a faintly bearded but Disney-eyed martini baby of what passed locally for a wealthy Jewish industrialist. She had left town a demi-vierge and stopped writing. Grasping at straws, as they say, Tom had taken up the piano, only to be left more desolate than ever from being unable to touch the source of the vibes, to feel the ridges of his big fingerprints scraping against something tangible at the top of the sound envelope.

The blatant sensuality of the impulse had manifestly been endorsed by Our Heavenly Father Himself when Tom's Episcopalian godmother fell down three flights of stairs that very month, bashed her skull open, puked and died, and bequeathed him exactly the right amount of money for a bottom-of-the-line piece of garbage from Lyon & Healy. (That's another tantalizing instrumental hint: they only make one kind.)

The various other burnt-out fellow cub-entheonauts amongst young Tom's classmates became suicides, practitioners of alternate sexual polarities or, in extreme cases, rabbis. Tom, on the other hand, played *harp* for a few years. That's right: harp. You can switch to the other side of this flip book now. I'll understand.

To realize that I was performing professionally after only two bumblings of our planet around our frumpy little star is to be tempted to assume I had talent, instead of the central nervous equivalent of a gaping wound whose ragged tissues hankered to stick and scab onto whatever band aid came near. Hence my selection of the western repertoire's gauziest instrument. It helped to be an aesthetically sociopathic thief and adulterer of other people's music. And it also helped to have an audience barbarous in the first instance: Donny and Marie Osmond worshippers, intent not on delectating harmonies and melodies, but rather on inhaling trenchers of rustic deep Crisco-fried hanta-viral rodent gristle and washing the greasy pathology down with tepid Sanka.

Now, at the time I am fondly reminiscing about, the Telestial Spaw was going through an identity crisis similar to Tom Bradley's own. The Glassy Cock had been debating in his heart whether or not to switch this place to a private club and apply for a liquor-by-the-drink license. Which clientele to cultivate: the mob of steadfast, loyal, but uninteresting Latter Day Saints, or the few dozen rich atheists and shining Jewish sophisticates from down in Salt Lake City, who seemed to have developed a health fad, a mineral-bathing craze among themselves?

Such a well-maintained Spaw attracted not only brown beauties in swimming suits of odd and non-functional shapes, but also the pale, sullen, tragic, barren, wasted women of the intelligentsia: the sort who held their Eve cigarettes up around their earlobes, displaying with unconscious pride the emaciated state of their forearms, exhaling smoke through their effete nostrils (one of which was generally plugged up), looking straight at you with evident disrelish while they scratched themselves. Sophisticates though they may have been, how they would have blushed to hear what the rubes they patronized got up to in the Private Bath.

Some of them wore tee shirts instead of bikini tops, and these tee shirts bore the then-newish motto, "A woman without a man is like a fish without a bicycle." Of course, the house harpist was too terrified to tell them the first juvenile response that popped into his contrary mind, something about seafood-reeking seats. He could be arch and insouciant when he played his transcriptions for empty-headed bathing beauties, but not in front of these bland intelligentsiatrices: they made him self-conscious about the angle at which he was holding his eyebrows.

Eyebrow hyper-awareness distracted from manual awareness, and made the unhappy house harpist fuck Mozart even worse than usual. This, I like to believe, had a deleterious effect on my forlorn campaign to get the beautiful bus girl with the flaring nostrils to act interested, and perhaps even to think of me and the Secret Sex Pot in a single steamy mental breath.

On the other hand, how fastidious could a habitue of such a place be? Aside from all the unfortunate rural-Utah odors, the sinusy mineral bath smells, the goat-crotch, crushed-skunk and horse diarrhea smells, the vestigial whiffs of volcanic sulfur, which permeated the atmosphere of the whole resort, the only other thing that reminded you that you were in the savage provinces of the Rocky Mountain West was the floor plan of the main building.

This had been designed many generations before by those geothermal barn-minded Scandinavian converts, and was laid out in such a way that the men's echoing showers, full of the inevitable pubescent boys shrieking arias, were within earshot of the opulent and ponderous dining room, with its mead-hall-from-Beowulf decor, its twelve-point antler racks and Volkswagen-sized stuffed grizzly heads, its heraldic displays of early Mormon death instruments, its mighty roof beams, and its big blazing stone fireplace with an archetypal lyre perched under the granite mantlepiece, embraced by a huge and brooding *Flaming Seraph* (that's what I had sequined across the sound box in Wayne Newton font). How drastically the buffet ambience contrasted with that of the Private Bath I am in no position to report. My presence in the latter chamber of delights was strictly analogue.

The sun-flaked bull of a female lifeguard, who happened to double as Mrs. Glasscock-Five, had periodically to bellow throughout the Telestial Spaw a scrannel "Let's us keep it down in them shaw'rs, hey," using the same voice with which she invoked Death within the bowels of pony Purgatory. And the aria-shrieking pubescent boys–not without justification (who ever heard of a silent shower? If he wanted silent showers, Mr. Glasscock should've removed all this satisfying aquamarine tile and lined the place with cork)–treated the diners to booming, crystal-clear retorts of "Why don't you come in here, Mrs. Lifeguard-Lady, and suck my cock, hah? Come on, it's right he-e-e-ere, m-m-my cock, my cock, my co-o-o-ock?" (to the tune of "Celeste Aida").

And the white-haired Mormon diners, who had just finished ut-tering "Heavenly Father bless you" in complete seriousness to a coreli-gionist, would perform an abrupt *subito* and hold their calico serviettes to their lips as if to dab away the taste of soaped pre-teen penises.

Now, when Mr. Glasscock wasn't having his ass figuratively kissed by the likes of me and Augie the Stable Master and the beautiful bus girl with the flaring nostrils, he was having it literally kissed in his quality as Baphomet of the Private Bath. But this did nothing to decrease the impression of abashed pudency which he gave off as he moved among the tables like the sacramental celebrant he was beneath the surface, consoling his guests with broad arm gestures, calling everybody's attention away from the shower racket and toward the brilliant instrumentalist whom he'd possessed the informed taste to engage for their edification.

Meanwhile, Tom's hourly forty-five-minute break would have rolled around, causing him to abandon harp and bugged music stand and vanish in the direction of Shitland Pony Hell. Rather than allow the customers to digest to the rhythm of cock arias, Mr. Glasscock would press a special button that brought the blessings of broadcast radio to the Telestial Spaw's P.A. system.

V.

God gave us music so that we, first and foremost, will be guided upward by it. All qualities are united in music: it can lift us up, it can be capricious, it can cheer us up and delight us, nay, with its soft, melancholy tunes, it can even break the resistance of the toughest character. Its main purpose, however, is to lead our thoughts upward, so that it elevates us, even deeply moves us. ... Music also provides pleasant entertainment and saves everyone who is interested in it from boredom. All humans who despise it should be considered mindless, animal-like creatures. Ever be this most glorious gift of God my companion on my life's journey, and I can consider myself fortunate to have come to love it. Let us sing out in eternal praise to God who is offering us this beautiful enjoyment.

–Nietzsche (age fourteen),
Über Musik

The orgiasts in the Private Bath are slumped in a post-orgasmic stupor, having neglected to press the STOP button on their ghetto blaster. The cassette tape continues to play, even after the house harpist has botched the cadence of the Mozart selection that climaxes his program with a whimper.

Augie and I now hear, over the usual ambient din, instead of Euterpean travesties, 50,000-watt clear-channel KSL Radio. It starts to blare over the sound system, to occupy the space between people's ears the harp has vacated. The Glassy Cock has read in a qualitative marketing textbook that customers tend to ingest to the rhythm of their aural environment, whatever it may be; and the Telestial Spaw has been firmly committed to the concept of Rapid High-Volume Patron Turnover ever since the early days of Grandfather Glasscock, the pioneer founder who grabbed this suppurating scab of earth from an extended family of Uncompahgres, Augie's ancestors. The application of this greasy-spoon hash-house "marketing strategy" juxtaposes oddly well with the supposed elegance of the place itself.

I am always conscientious about starting my break at the top of the hour, in order to hear the local news blasted out over the heads of my chomping audience–

"The badly decomposed, partially dismembered–"

"Would you folks care to enjoy your cream of asparagus soup now or later?"

"–sexually molested, nude-from-the-waist-down, bloated corpse of a retarded–"

"I'll take the tomato omelette, please. Keep it darn runny. I like the way the mucousy stuff soaks into the oaken grain of your rustic trenchers. Makes me feel real handcart-pioneer-like. And, li'l Missy, what you going to have?"

"–covered with human bite marks, was found floating in Moroni Reservoir this morning. The sheriff's office reports having arrested a local duly elected neighborhood 'bishop' on suspicion of ritually–"

They swallow on, these patrons, desensitized to such things, in much the same way that their sons and daughters and grandchildren, even unto the *nth* generation, keep shoveling in the popcorn and Ju-jus at a PG-rated movie downtown, while Robert Redford's screen-colleagues slash each other with voluptuous motions and die and bleed, snuggling up to the ground, sighing.

After the weather and Dow Jones industrial averages, the boys resume their sudsy cock arias and the Flaming Seraph re-mounts the stone hearth. From his station in front of the gas logs, he often improvises a tasteful accompaniment subtly to enhance and reflect the nuances of mood as he imagines them out there in the locker room.

Tom Bradley found himself imagining the showers and their humid atmosphere with very poignant feelings surfacing in his breast. But it must be emphasized that these feelings were in no way inspired by illicit thoughts of possessing the sleek young bodies that happened to be shrieking in there. Unfashionable or no, Tom was no pansy, no bloomer-button, no Nancy-boy. He was the kind of guy that would've picked Lot's virgin daughter over the two angel boys any day of the god-damned mother-fucking week. If those Sodomites had all been like this harpist, their town would never have been vaporized.

Rather, his hankerings were after all that cool, more or less clear, faucet water; for, in consideration of the remoteness of this Spaw, Tom had resigned himself to a showerless, gypsylike existence for as long as the gig lasted. And, considering the ripenings which occur when such a huge person lives like a showerless gypsy for any length of time, it was safe to assume that Tom didn't exactly enjoy an enviable level of job security, even in so pungent a restaurant.

But this may have been mere persecution mania on his part. The Glassy Cock never gave the slightest wince, not even a sidelong glance of disapproval, at Tom's poor grooming and worse odor. The old tantric adept was far too impressed with Tom's sheer technical mastery of his musical instrument to risk offending him with criticism of his personal hygiene.

Tom's boss did, however, occasionally beg him to brush his long orange tresses out a bit, and actually provided the brush every time. Then, strange to say, the little man would, with almost ritual reverence, take the implement back upon himself, its bristles interwoven with the dandruff and prematurely fallen hair of the Flaming Seraph.

And, as if moved to nervousness by this privilege, Mr. Glasscock would pause in silence, put his fingertips in his mouth, and begin methodically biting his nails to the quick. He'd save the ten scalloped moon-crescents, as was his habit, and stack them with care in the pocket of his leisure suit jacket like pre-fab potato chips. Then, admiring his unshampooed double fistful like a pirated cassette tape of heavenly music, he'd wander out to Augie's domain.

Gathering bits of your narrator's personal detritus for magickal purposes, eh? Religion can do terrible things to a man's personality.

VI.

...three-chord manure.
　　　　　　　–Mel Torme

My pal Augie has to talk pretty loudly, to be heard over the sick sacramental racket steaming yellowishly up between our feet.

"Page, Jimmy. You know. He's down there with the boss-prophet. Come on, man, get hep. Jimmy Page. He belongs to that top-ten Hit Parade pop-rock outfit. Jethro Tull and the Deltones, or whatever."

"Top-ten Hit Parade pop-rock outfit? Our town doesn't attract too many of those. Weren't they here six or seven years ago? Yeah, they composed us a major work–

Down in Utah
The guys and I dig a city called Salt La-a-a-ake.
It's got the grooviest kids
That's why we never get tired of Salt La-a-a-ake.
And the way the kids talk so cool
Is an out of sight thing,
Yeah...
Salt Lake Cityyyyyyyyy, we'll be coming sooooon..."

"That's the Beach Bitches. Stop screeching. You'll stampede the pygmy ponies. No, he belongs to one of those foreign top-ten pop-rock outfits. Like, um–"

"Dave Clark Five."

"Yeah. No. Fuck. He's down there talking to Prophet-Seer-Revelator Glasscock. I think he's trying to persuade the old man to sell him—"

"Pay no attention to the mope behind the travertine."

Much to my chagrin, enough to start dragging me down into a bum trip, on the cassette tape I seem to be back on the job, segueing to the most embarrassing number in my humiliating repertoire: Mozart's Concerto for Flute, Harp and Orchestra in C Major, KV 299.

VII.

Mozart was treated with a strange mixture of mistrust and fear.

–Bruno Manz, *Memoir of a Son and Soldier of the Third Reich*

Believe it or not, despite my lysergic butchery at the Telestial Spaw Pioneer-Style Steam Buffet, that egregious piece of Age of Enlightenment schmalz holds a most illustrious place in the annals of psychedelia. The first LSD writing of all time was conceived to the accompaniment of its excessive tunefulness.

How is that possible? The composer himself, had he been acquainted with Albert Hofmann's "problem child," would be more puzzled than any of us. The ex-wunderkind of Number 9 Getreidegasse was clearly on nothing resembling an acid trip, good or bad, when, with little thought and less bother, he dashed the piece off for his high-born patron, Adrien-Louis de Bonnières, the Duke of Guînes—one of those eternal Glasscock types to whom the likes of him and me are karma-fucked to owe mortality's continuance.

Given the most superficial exposure to this flabby and paradoxically unMozartean noise, it's possible, even for the untrained ear, the barbarous ear, the transfat- and cerumen-compacted auditory meatus (and there are plenty of those around the Telestial Spaw), to divine not only the character but the physique of the patron who ordered, though only half paid for, the *Flarpathon* (as it's unaffectionately known among us non-chicken pluckers). I've always wondered, if only fifty percent of the promised fee was forthcoming, which half went unpaid for? If it was the harp part, maybe I can knock off early and we can all flip over and enjoy *Dr. Gonzo*.

Listen through the travertine to the Flarpathon's opening theme as it jiggles like sebaceous cellulite layered in dimples on thighs that prance in gold lame brocade tights. You will synaestheticize with your tympanic eyes someone morbidly obese, yet a bangled dandy for all his surplus avoirdupois. Like so many moneyed walruses, the Duke of Guînes, Adrien-Louis de Bonnières, suffers from a peacock complex proportional to his girth. If he wasn't costumed like an Eighteenth Century blue-blood, you'd swear Mozart's stingy Glasscock in this instance was a contemporary American, swilling Sanka and simpering grace to *Heav'nly Faw-w-w-wther* at the Telestial Spaw Pioneer-Style Steam Buffet. (I'm wise in my programming.)

Though his budgetary concerns denied Mozart much more than two *kreutzer* to rub together, you'll be relieved to learn that the Duke of Guînes, Adrien-Louis de Bonnières, was able to muster the wherewithal to have two pairs of breeches tailored for each of his resplendent suits of clothes. Every morning his secretary would scrutinize the schedule and determine if it was to be a stand-up or sit-down day. Tight breeches were prescribed for the former, loose for the latter. A man doesn't achieve such prosperous proportions without a festering oral fixation. And this douche–excuse me, duke–just happens to have been the flautist in our rudimentary equation. I bet you can guess who was saddled–rather, played the saddle–to the other solo instrument.

It's likely *le duc* considered a daughter, like tight breeches, to be nothing more or less than a beautification of his inflated presentation self. Hence his causing Mozart to teach his penis-unencumbered offspring to play a golden instrument possessing more furniture value than musical utility. The daughter of a duke is entitled to be called "Lady" no matter how simian her brow or prognathous her jaw. And, even though she was no older than our bus girls, *my Lady* is how Mozart was obliged to address the no-talent slag during their private lessons together.

As you suffer through the concerto commissioned as a vehicle for this Oedipal pairing, please wince in sympathy for Mozart. Hear him plumb such abysses of boredom as only rare genius can spelunk, particularly in the Andantino. I never knew the bowels conducted their own peristalsis till this slow torture stopped mine each brunch time in the demon-rife desert of my teens. One can just picture the Beloved of God's guts also paralyzing with each delayed twitch of the metronome.

"Girlfriend," he seems to moan, "you daughter of first cousins, who have taught me the meaning of the phrase *hybrid vigor*–why are you so sluggishly autoeroticizing this dildo twixt your tween twat? At your age you should be dashing around causing trouble like the Contessa's naughty chambermaid in the new comic opera which I'd like to get back to work on, if you'll only die of sudden apoplexy, please, my *La-a-a-a-a-ady*,"

Maybe now you can begin to forgive my erstwhile reluctance to burden this half of our flip book with the H-word. Nobody with more than subnormal levels of neural organization would come within a single index finger's width of this glorified egg slicer, this Rube Goldberg maze of pedals and clamps and attenuated strands of feline digestive tract. Anyone with half an eardrum and no financial interest would react like a garlicked Bela Lugosi to its sour mockery of well-temperedness.

These days, on this stupid piece of spaz crap, to which my livelihood has been chained like Prometheus to the Caucasian crag, when I want a sharp or a flat I need to stomp a stocking foot on one of seven pedals that peek ever so coquettishly out from amongst the cheap gold leafing at my tootsies. But if, like a porn star, you can suppress your autonomic gag reflex, force your mind to feature the following notion: the Eighteenth-Century harp was even more fucked.

It could only play sharps, no flats, so the harmonic possibilities were choked like a chicken. Mozart tried to make up for the imposed tedium by jigger-rigging a disproportionately large number of catchy melodic motifs, much like a screenwriter who has access neither to omniscience nor soliloquy to speak of, and must rely on superficial sights and sounds to earn his beans for the day.

That's why the diatonically cretinous Flarp-Flop winds up being the last piece in my luncheon buffet set. I save it for when I am getting fatigued. After rendering, say, a Bach transcription with a counter-subject constituting a descending chromatic scale, my stocking feet ache, for they have been writhing faster among the pedals than my thumbs have finger-fornicated the forty-two or -nine strings (I never counted). At such times, being constitutionally phlegmatic, I yearn for the slot in the program reserved for this cretinous novelty item.

My lower body can almost vegetate, and my feet can behave as if chained to a cozy dungeon floor, like a top-ten Hit Parade pop-rocker who has only three chords to "think about," so to speak—even though I'm holding down the flute as well as my own harp part and the orchestral *tutti*, more or less, sort of. The score calls for two oboes, two French horns and a moderately large load of strings to back up the soloists, but that's child's play compared to, say, the Chou Dynasty Festival Orchestra's ten thousand cats wailing on 300 different kinds of axes. (I would wind up shot in the back of the neck in China.) It helps to have fingers so long that, when not making racket, they can palm a buttered basketball with just the ridges of the mutant fingerprints engaged, plenty of daylight between the fortune-telling bits and the tawny rubber nubbles.

Mozart didn't bother to write any cadenzas for either flute or harp (both of which gizmos he openly loathed and only went near when gulden were promised), so it's a chance for me to kill some paid time without even pretending to make music: lots and lots of random glissandi dignified as "improvised." Especially on acid I feel like a whore, or maybe a duke, dipped in peacock puke.

With that sensation in mind, please hear our particular solar system's very first acid writing, as inspired by this self-same Concerto for Flute, Harp and *agga-blagga-gagga*—

*A blue plume ascended from the tip of the [incense] stick.
He looked at it first with astonishment, then with delight,
as if a new power of the eyes had come to him. It revealed
itself in the play of this fragrant smoke, which ascended
from the slender stick and then branched out into a delicate
crown. It was as if his imagination had created it—a pallid
web of sea lilies in the depths, that scarcely trembled from
the beat of the surf.*

That comes from the purplish pen of a war-worshiping
hater of democracy and loather of Hebrews, a Mut und Tod
cultist, a zillion-times wounded World War One hero and Iron
Cross honoree who, though courted slavishly as a national
treasure by the Nazis, treated Hitler with disdain and possibly
even pitched in on the plot to assassinate him—but only as a
tiresome vulgarian upstart.

What does this tell you about psychedelic scribbling?
Imagine what could be written by a modest, unintoxicated,
pacifistic philosemite listening to an actual symphony.

Hear the remainder of the quotation—

*Time was active in this creation—it had circled it, whirled
about it, wreathed it, as if imaginary coins rapidly piled
up one on top of another. The abundance of space revealed
itself in the fiber work, the nerves, which stretched and
unfolded in the height, in a vast number of filaments.*

So, who do you reckon quilled this great-grampappy of
all acid writing, to the lilting strains of earwaxy Q-tip fluff
Mozart twiddled with one harmonic hand tied behind his
back in return for pocket money that wound up being mostly
unforthcoming?

In approximately the same temporal neighborhood that
saw the commencement of my genethliacal horoscopy, our
man Ernst Junger was contacted by Albert Hofmann and

recruited to come on over to the house for the "first planned psychedelic test." The latter was confident that the former, an entheonaut since the early years of the twentieth century, would be persuaded to eat some of the "new *phantasticum*," especially if the host promised to put some tunes on the phonograph and gussy up the experience in other ways.

What they dropped wasn't cartooned on tiny squares of blotter paper, and did not compare in other ways to the chartreuse goat that muddles my teen-boy thoughts in the Righteous Wrangler Riding Stable. Their stuff was, by definition, more than ultra-connoisseur-quality. It was the first hearty burgundy Dionysus ever strained between his toes; it was the original Soma, the good stuff that made for a cleanly and wholesome drunk, before the identity of the secret ingredient was forgotten, and the Rig Vedic Indra could get rat-assed with sublime dignity. (We will soon see the irony of Hofmann's Vedic *phantasticum* being wasted on Junger's post-Vedic nature.)

A trip was prepared to please even the snootiest would-be *aristo-kratisch* palate. The arrangement of ambiance was just as impeccable as the chemical constitution of the intoxicant. For all his Blut und Boden blustering against bourgeois complacency, Herr Storm and Steel surrendered his hallucinogenic cherry in comfy-snug conditions. Listen to Hofmann, who sounds like Mark Helprin being interviewed at Salon.com–

> We gathered in the fashionable living room, with dark wooden ceiling, white tile fireplace, period furniture, old French engravings on the walls, a gorgeous bouquet of tulips on the table.

Simply gorgeous. No mention is made of flooring, but I feel safe assuming it leaned further toward the Persian rug end of the spectrum than the manure and straw which I now tread in a parallel trip with my own gracious host. (I'm Ernie,

Augie is Al.) As for costume, I frankly don't care to contrast the dacron polyester stage-drag Mr. Glasscock forces me to wear with my predecessor's duds, which are catalogued as follows:

> *Ernst Junger wore a long, broad, dark blue striped kaftan-like garment that he had brought from Egypt. The everyday reality should be laid aside, along with everyday clothing.*

You can see how an elegant gold-leaf furniture piece would fit right in. Indeed, I am beginning to wonder if the Duke of Guînes, Adrien-Louis de Bonnières, might have been floating around Hofmann's parlor in spirit–but not his daughter, for they were also fastidious in their selection of animate accompaniment.

Herr Professor-Doktor Hofmann told any and all screwy broads to vacate the premises before the acid started taking effect. Only one head trip at a time for these brilliant yet narcissistic Aryans, with their low pigmentation egos draped in the sort of post-Prussian brass and bangles that appear so gay to an Anglo Saxon eye such as mine. Unlike my boss in the Private Bath, they preferred no Kali avatar to be present, no yowling Crowleyite Splinter-Mormon crone. Nor was there a beautiful bus girl to flare nostrils over this steamed brain buffet.

Latter Day Saints may funk the hot drink, but not Ernie and Al. "The old chronicles," explains Hofmann, "described how the Aztecs drank *chocolatl* before they ate *teonanacatl*. Thus [my *Hausfrau*] served us hot chocolate, to set the mood. Then she abandoned the men to their fate."

So much for four of the five senses. But what condescending conclusions can we draw regarding the tympanic membranes of our two old dope fiends of yesteryear? Maybe none. Perhaps the *Flöte- und Harfekonzert* was the only phonograph record Hofmann could find around the house with no Jewish involvement. Despite the honored guest's disdain for *unsere israelitische Brüder*, that no less fastidious than talented tribe were busy in the fifties, as now, mounting performances of proper Mozart—for example, the Jupiter Symphony (which we will consider presently). Check any number of album notes, keeping in mind what you have learned from the preceding pages of our flip book, and you will not be astonished at the over-whelmingly *goyische* personnel on harp records.

These two prepuce-encumbered *Schweineschnitzel*-eaters listened to the most embarrassing thing I ever did with my hands (which is saying a lot). And, according to the Father of LSD, they "perceived its celestial beauty as heavenly music." Both Ernie and Al lived into their hundreds, just as no small number of my auditors at the Spaw exhibited a stereotypically Mormon longevity inexplicable in the context of their diabetes-baiting dietary habits. One can only suspect some salubrious quality in such one-hand-tied-behind-the-back Muzak.

However, its effect on the wallet is more problematic. If poor Mozart was tossed no more than a *pfennig* or two for releasing these sounds into the air, I milked the piece for an hourly wage that, I am proud to reveal, put all but the most senior bus girls to shame. Seeing as how a goodly percentage of my wage went to LSD purchases, and considering how absurdly cheap that concoction still was in those days, the 200-plus-year-old relationship of the Flarpathon to lucre is worth examining now.

VIII.

I don't know what friend of yours I've killed, I don't know what child of yours I've hurt, I don't know what food I've taken out of your mouth...but these jokes about me will stop, and they'll stop now. Or I will kick your ass.
                                            —Wayne Newton

"We're mere entertainers is all."

Musicians of all sorts, particularly when they are within smelling range of lucre, have been known to shuck and jive and say that. Even Mozart allowed similar sentiments to slip his lips when it served to disarm the moneyed bastards who fed him, or didn't. There's always a direct ratio between the apparent vehemence of the assertion and the amount of lucre it might snag.

And, in the context of lucre, who's the greatest "mere entertainer" of our age? Why, none other than the highest paid act in lizard lounge history: Wayne Newton, crooner of this chapter's epigraph. He's at the peak of his preternatural powers this junior year of my high school career.

Just watch that Big Bertha don his sequined tux and work the Imperial Deluxe Room at Nero's Golden Whore Boudoir on the Fabulous Las Vegas Strip. He gets the band vamping along, then bestirs his ambiguous self setting up a row of folding chairs along the brim of the stage, upon which he plunks an array that can only be called dazzling: banjo, accordion, bass clarinet, glockenspiel, Jew's harp, English horn, handsaw with rubber mallet, dulcimer, viola da gamba, theorbo, kazoo, and so forth. (No harp, incidentally, because it would only confirm the rumors that he's a hermaphrodite.) Then he goes down the line and plays a solo on each one more expertly than the previous, bringing down the house with his sonic juggling act.

This creepily indiscriminate serial intimacy with inanimate objects stems, no doubt, from some genetic deficiency in the propriocentric centers of the brain-body: overcompensation for alienation from every bit of self above the wrists, behind the embouchure, and from the ass both ways. Have you ever seen that guy walk? Come to think of it, maybe my instrument's absent from Mr. *Danke Schoen*'s arsenal because it involves the feet.

By the time his dimpled pinkies reach for the climactic tuba, all the old ladies' underpants have sailed onto his padded shoulders, where they sop and drain the sort of witchy ichor that flows this evening in the Private Bath. The unpantied crones give that pudgy morfadyke the sort of ovation formerly reserved for the twenty-four month-old Mozart when, blindfolded, earplugged, bound in in silken mittens, suspended upside-down from the ceiling, he improvised seven-part *prestissimo* fugues on a harpsichord with Marie Antoinette's moist personal linen covering the keys.

As for the narrator of the present side of our flip book– where does he come down in this dialectic? He can barely propriocentralize himself through a doorway without bumping his head or twisting a hyper-extended knee. But he can lay self-alienated hands on a mute contraption and, in two years, cause it to make sounds which, albeit hideous, are more articulate than what issues from vocal tracts ordering brunch at the Telestial Spaw. He can play a smaller number of instruments than Wayne, but for a slightly longer period of time, without boring an audience no less moronic than the Vegas clientele (or the Versailles for that matter), but unstupefied by alcohol and tobacco. That tallies up to make Tom Bradley the slightly superior musician. I mean superior to Wayne, but probably not Wolfgang.

This is important because, like so many teen-boys at that time who were too large, rubicund and *goyische* to pass as Bob Dylan clones, I had a hunch that I was more or less physically repulsive, in a Newtonian sort of way. And we middle-class deracinated Anglo Saxons are in any case brought up by our harpy moms to assume that accomplishment brings love, not intrinsic lovableness.

And, speaking of repulsiveness and moms and brought love, no child labor laws needed breaking to bring the beautiful bus girl with the flaring nostrils into my life, for she was an older woman, all of twenty-one. She was a peaches-and-cream complexioned native of the desert, most likely nurtured on the vocal talents of Ernest Tubb and Cowboy Copas. She probably wouldn't know a *fugato* passage from a clogged sinus passage. And she wasn't interested in the burlesque figure we've provisionally named Tom Bradley, anyway. She just loitered around his fireplace during brunch because it was the only cranny where the ingratiating old cashier, one of Mr. Glasscock's putative plural grandmothers, couldn't see or smell her smoking.

Rube this beautiful bus girl with the flaring nostrils was, but she'd also been nurtured on television, and she knew how to make her surface sparkle, glint and cut like an ice-blue diamond. She could've just that morning descended, all oily and musky, from the swankiest of penthouses in the hugest of metropolises, the sleaziest of saxophones moaning pelvic-sounding slurs on the soundtrack.

But it could never be, thought Tom, dejected. An unbridgeable gap yawned between their respective milieux. Her career in the food services industry was one long observation of the dictates of table etiquette, while Tom liked nothing so much as curling up on the travertine with a raw cauliflower.

His bus girl's name was Peri, and perhaps she was a peri down on her luck. While the Flaming Seraph sat upon his stone pedestal never breaking a sweat, Peri was up to her depilated armpits in used food-matter: the gnawed skeletons of deep-fried hanta virus rodents pulled from that "crick" right outside the window (actually a kind of New World micro-wadi scraped by a flash flood when the sky allowed us some fluid a couple generations or so ago).

Garbage-coated, Peri would saturate herself with Xanaduian Mood Musk Number Nine, or something like that. And, somehow, clear through her endless shift, she'd manage to maintain a breezy, toothy, elegant, cool smile, an inscrutable squint of sophisticated mirth, big tip-garnering. It only went away at those moments when the Flaming Seraph, from behind his sequined instrument, said something seductive or observant of the truth—or maybe a combination of both, like, "Hey Peri! That meat you're fetching back 'n forth looks like somebody's dog already ate it!"

At those moments, her streamlined risible muscles would relax into honest, attractive loathing, just for the tiniest of seconds. She would cluck a high involuntary "Oh!" and pause, then resume her professional grimace of a smile, as if to say, "I'll ignore that one. But from now on I'm keeping a tally. And don't expect to catch me off guard again. Don't expect me to relax my lovely, cool smile any more no matter what you do, for I am prepared now. And, as for accompanying you and your ten thumbs to the Secret Sex Pot, well, let's just say I suspect not."

So he unwedged the harp and whipped out his scrotum.

No, he didn't. What he did was back off like a whipped puppy, tacitly promising to watch his tongue from now on. Occasionally, though, this giant house harpist would make a comeback, right in Peri's perfect face. For example, one time he couldn't find his regular sturdy aluminum stool, so deployed one of the elegant Telestial Corporation dining room chairs to the business end of his dick substitute and, fittingly enough, sat down. It splintered and collapsed under him. Fortunately, by virtue of the uncanny reaction time that many pathologically slothful people seem to enjoy, and by dint of thigh muscles overdeveloped from pedaling Bach and trying to pedal Schoenberg for so many years, he was able to catch himself in mid-fall, avoiding the inconvenience and embarrassment of the fractured sacroiliac, and he saved himself to out-Wayne Wayne Newton another day.

While still hovering in the sitting position, Tom flipped his newly-brushed hair out of his eyes and sighed with infinite languor. With six-inch-long pinkies fastidiously curled, he reached down and selected a fragment of splintered chair. This he held up and examined delicately as a deep-fried rodent leg. Then, still seated on thin air, Tom delivered himself of some gnome comment or other in a mincing, swishy urban Mormon accent, a la their boss.

Weakly heaving his labio-velars, he said something like, "Well, shall we say it's not exactly one of the artifacts that, millennia hence, will serve to represent late-twentieth-century North American cul-ture?"

His bus girl, loitering at his feet and cupping a cigarette in her left hand, was just perceptibly nonplussed. She recovered, did her little soprano "cluck," and made some short, grinning putdown. This was drowned out by a screaming infant that had been lugged in and dumped on a nearby table like a half-choked chicken. Tom asked her to go stick a fork in it and see if it was done.

In his desire to squelch her smirk, Tom perhaps gave the impression that he wasn't overly fond of the younger set. Nothing could have been further from the truth. There was nothing more agreeable to the Flaming Seraph than being surrounded by squirming, tumbling babies during one of his sets. He liked it when they danced or sang or percussed along with the flatware; and he encouraged them by peeking between the titty mags on his music stand and pulling cross-eyed clown faces when their parents weren't looking. If these infantile fans' tiny fingers had been capable of manipulating safety pins, they would have flung their diapers, just as Wayne's Vegas ladies did their panties.

With enough post-fetal background noise, the minority of diners who were interested would not be able to hear that the maestro in their midst never tuned his hypertrophied ukulele. When no loud kids were around, he was forced to play his ugly Berio and Hindemith into the deathly quiet, because there were more notes his thumbnails could blunder into without it sounding as though he'd made a mistake.

But, no matter how horribly its strings are scraped, this particular type of instrument sounds at least unobnoxious to a sufficiently stupid auditor. And, most of the time on the job, the sweetness of Tom's harp turned him, like the sweetness of his flute turned Goldsmith, into the fey and tranquil sort, willing to look around and derive simple pleasure from his neighboring organisms.

For instance, Tom loved the fifteen-year-old bus girls, those who shied away like unbroken ponies from anything in pants, yet who seemed to have been born with eyes and ears for no other reason than to pick up pointers from older females in the art of sexual allurement and subtle repelling. They gathered and watched so blatantly when someone they admired, like Peri, stepped forward to deal with a male, any male, a cowhand or groundskeeper, or even a musician.

Typical rural Mormonettes, Tom's virgin co-workers were doomed to teen marriage in a matter of months, and to unceasing pregnancy till menopause. Most of them would never unwrap a Tampax in their lives. In the meantime, Tom made free to admire these menial bus girls' unfoaled body-woddies: cross between bony and baby-pudge soft, long-legged and clumsy, big-footed like puppies, yet somehow capable of defying gravity, eager to lift off at any moment.

And he loved the way they touched each other on forearms and smalls of backs while giggling and gossiping over a tableful of garbage, and how quickly they swallowed their silly smiles when they realized that the harpist from the city was observing them. They shot him serious, pouting looks that resembled so much loathing.

70

He would shift into pianissimo and overhear these mustard moppers' flutey voices on break time as they discussed ways to make time fly on the job: "You just sorta switch off your brain, y'know? And play like your arms and hands is a machine that works itself."

This was the man who, in his own pampered life, was trying to suck time dry, to make every minute a three-day weekend; yet he found it almost agonizingly charming to hear these uneducated child-laborers sigh in contentment over the shift's last table.

"Gol, that was a fast day. Wish they could all go that fast."

The only question was how much time they spent in the Private Bath, and how fast it went.

IX.

It is stated in the holy scriptures or books, dear lady, that there exists a race of daimons who have commerce with women. Hermes made mention of them in his Physika; in fact almost the entire work, openly and secretly, alludes to them. It is related in the ancient and divine scriptures that certain angels lusted for women, and descending from the heavens, they taught them all the arts of nature. On account of this, says the scripture, they offended god, and now live outside heaven—because they taught to men all the evil arts which are of no advantage to the soul.

—Zosimos of Panopolis

Tantrism in its spermo-gnostic and quasi-Kabbalistic manifestations floated over our wasteland like unshampooed crotch-stench. It wafted after dark on curdled cream-colored clouds of sulfur from oaken cracks in the portal which Glasscock's perversity had caused to be countersunken in the Righteous Wrangler Riding Stable's shadowy back wall. And, as I stand with the master of that stable and feel the green blotter soak up my awareness, I'm sorry to report that bodily products even more fragrant than those of a reproductive nature are blended into the nasal bouquet.

But perhaps that particular stench-flavor is appropriate, considering the shitty music with which our resident Crowleyites have chosen to serenade the Dark Goddess of these Latter Days. Even my poor pal Augie, congenitally polite as most full-blooded Uncompahgres, is having a hard time maintaining composure under the tape-recorded barrage of me perverting the already perverse Concerto for Flute, Harp and Orchestra in C Major, KV 299.

Augie tries his best to prevent his semi-civilized, therefore vivid imagination from visualizing the uncircumcised knob that we both can reluctantly hear knocking against the back of the ghetto blaster. That contrivance has been tied, codpiece-wise, with anti-consecrated, leftward-spun horsehair twine, around the puckered, undraped love handles of one of Mr. Glasscock's superannuated acolyte-flunkies. This is done for some esoteric reason with which I'm not karmically incontinent enough to familiarize myself. As Iamblichus of old so rightly cautions us—

> *It is necessary to know the nature of this wonder-making art, but by no means have faith in it.*

Tonight's Bearer of the Tunes happens to be our Rural Free Delivery mailman, who only passed the civil service exam thanks to connections Mr. Glasscock enjoys at the higher levels of terrestrial authority. Flunky-acolytes do pretty much anything the boss tells them, even to the point of taking their turn ceremoniously galumphing your narrator's cassette-taped cacophony round and round the conjure circle, like some labor-intensive version of Quadrophony or Sensurround (hot new innovations this year). The hope is that someday these lackeys will have curried enough faux-Satanic favor to be allowed bridally to breech an extra mini-wife or two among the indentured bus girls who toil elbow-to-elbow with me at the Telestial Spaw Pioneer-Style Steam Buffet.

It might be reassuring for you to be told that our bus girls are not sent into the soul's shredder-compactor without some gesture toward preparing them mentally—to the limited extent that adverb pertains in their context. The only problem is that Mr. Glasscock has taken it upon himself to provide the schooling personally, and his sense of audience is only slightly less delusional than that, say, of a harpist who tries to render Mozart for simian Utahns.

I once overheard our Prophet-Seer-Employer attempting to tutor an uncomprehending gaggle of nubile bussy girly-poos during their break time behind the flapping aluminum kitchen doors. He started out well enough, I suppose: "My daughters, open now your hearts and ears that you may gain understanding..." But then he got all preeny and went into a rant that suggested rote. He reminded me of an acid-addled Ernie barking Teutonicisms in Al's fashionable parlor, if a deep Crisco fryer and pancake griddle could be substituted for the *dark wooden ceiling*, the *white tile fireplace*, the *period furniture*, the *old French engravings*, and the *gorgeous bouquet of tulips on the table*.

Listen to my boss preach in a voice that the paranoiac in me suspects of being intended less for the little garbage gatherers than for the big eavesdropper on the other side of the kitchen flappers–

"Left-hand Tantric yogins on the Indian subcontinent disported themselves with the techniques of sex magic for ten underground centuries under the conquering Aryan civilization, and for untold millennia before that, among the indigenous Indus Valley folk. The ancient left path rites seeped up from the autochthonous Mohenjo-Daro and remained a persecuted underground tendency throughout the classical period, only to emerge in the Medieval. These formalized profundities were aped secondhand by Jews in their later Kabbalistic sex-magical workings, based on invidious observation of their Aryan captors' behaviors in the Babylonian sojourn. But no matter what its immediate cultural context, our universal furtive tradition, our undercurrent of transgressive erotic magic, tends to eucharize through the ritual secretion, excretion, manipulation and ingestion of so-called *polluting substances*."

Now comes a pause, during which this bibliophile braves the kitchen's deep Crisco steam, just as he braves the sulphurous fumes in the Private Bath, and starts waving around a priceless copy of some pertinent revealed scripture or other. In this case it would be the original 1898 edition of *White Stains*, personally signed and ejaculated upon by the author, one of seventeen crispy copies that miraculously escaped pulping at the sticky hands of Her Majesty Queen Victoria's customs agents. It's a remarkable tome by any standards; but I can't imagine why Mr. Glasscock expects it to get more of a reaction from American teens than any other tome, with or without glamorous jizz chips.

Where, by the way, you might wonder, does a Utahn get his hands on such a collectible? Aren't perquisites like these reserved for habitues of world capitals? Now do you believe me when I tell you my boss is no native? He's not handcart pioneer stock (unlike his star musician), but is rather a recent convert drawn to this biologically sterile yet spiritually fertile desert from a place no less distant than the spawning ground of those Hairy Ones who congregate and cry out in our salt and tar.

The fact that you hear no squeals of "Eeeew, gross!" at the manifestation of the Great Beast 666's mummified spermatozoa indicates just how fatuous Mr. Glasscock's sense of audience is. Nevertheless, undaunted, he presses on with his performance in the yawning, eye-rolling face of indifference, just as his house harpist must do each chow-time. We're troopers, the Prophet and I.

"I say *polluting*, girls, in the exoteric sense, and *terrific* in the esoteric sense, as in plumbing the terrible and terrifying mystery of coating spirits in skin, that miserable necessity. Our neo-Dravidian sacramental vintage is, as you see, semen. Our chrism is fornication's less specifiable fluidic discharges. Our unleavened wafer is the monthly clot—also known, in Crowleyan magick, as the *Elixir Rubeus*, which is semi-correctly considered by the graduate school of Freemasonry to be the Whore of Babylon's effluvium. And, my daughters, furthermore—"

The boistrous teen in me suddenly forgets the lowness of his rung on the Telestial Spaw career ladder. I open my mouth to yell, "As pick-up lines go, Glassy, it could use just a little—"

But then I feel a hand on my shoulder.

X.

As this spirit was doubtless a genuine elementary apparition, which made itself visible of its own free will—in short, an umbra—it was, as every respectable shadow should be, visible but impalpable, or if palpable at all, communicating to the feeling of touch the sensation of a mass of water suddenly clasped in the hand, or of condensed but cold steam. It was luminous and vapory...

–Madame Blavatsky,
Isis Unveiled

What happened next remained unclear in my memory till a quarter-century later, when I stumbled upon this passage in the *Chymical Wedding of Christian Rosenkreutz:*

> *...somebody in an unusual manner touched me on the back; whereupon I was so hugely terrified, that I durst hardly look about me...I looked back, and behold it was a fair and glorious lady...*

It was a tall, radiant being, the most beautiful creature I'd ever seen or imagined. Her face, hands and forearms were covered in skin that smelled and glowed like flowers with sun shining through them. For what seems, in memory, to have been a full minute, the beautiful bus girl with the flaring nostrils took me in through a pair of vast light-blue eyes. I was transfixed, like one of those doomed children at Fatima, long ago, who witnessed the Portuguese sun pop like a white phosphorus blister and splash down in the Atlantic.

It was as if she had manifested herself from billows of deep Crisco steam, seeping under the aluminum kitchen flappers just like the Shakti Avatar Kali doing the same from coagulated semen-colored sulphur vapors between oaken cracks in the Private Bath portal.

It was as though she'd been there all along, hovering invisibly behind my left shoulder, like Kali inverted, and only needed to be conjured by our Prophet-Seer-Revelator-Employer's voice, to resolve from the greasy dew. To say an uncomfortable moment passed is to talk geologically. Meanwhile, from the kitchen came the sound of Glasscock continuing to ply his pickup line–

"And, my children, working as you do within whiff and whinny distance of a tiny horse herd, can you now divine the occult meaning behind the legend that Ghengis Khan, the future subsister on spavined mare's milk, parturated clutching a motherly clot?"

–which, in turn, transmogrified into the cacophony of a sick musical instrument spinning round and round a conjure circle.

Peri's nostrils flared this time like those of a large feline carnivore, and her high "cluck" had become more of a sizzle, and she seemed to be drawing me by a handful of Glasscock's requisite dacron polyester in the direction of our Spaw Gawd's submerged noggin, the wilderness side, and the Secret Sex Pot concealed there.

And I recall, with equal vividity, a pair of contradictory responses on my part. You can believe one or the other, depending on whether the beautiful bus girl with the flaring nostrils, too, has overheard the boss and is aroused (in other words, she's a company girl), or whether she's heard nothing, and is aroused for some other reason which remains unimaginable.

In the first case I must now apologize and blush to admit that I fled headlong. I retreated to the safety of the Augean stable and LSD's eight-to-twelve-hour chemical neutering.

Alternatively, I will dive headfirst into the Secret Sex Pot and take a bath with this unwashed lumpenproletariette. We, the beautiful bus girl with the flaring nostrils and I, will be able to make out, by moonlight, yellow and white geysers between the weeds and vines and grass, froth coagulated in layers over its own layers over layers, gushing, tumbling. And the beautiful bus girl with the flaring nostrils, if she only consents, will be able to hear, along with me, the most delicate membranes of fizz and the coarsest belching globules, flashing moonlight inside white holes, rounded like pillows or lips, the travertine becoming translucent as grey sugar in the wet, bubble-scrubbed, dissolving places. Overhanging branches of peppermint, limp as cooked broccoli, and mint flowers, will foment and swell out from under their spiked buds, erupting pink lips, nervy, spear-shaped, languorously curled in the cream-tinted steam, dripping and hanging to poke or tickle the abdomen of a back-floating bather, there in the Secret Sex Pot, no reservation necessary.

And, at the end of the sex scene, she expresses a sentiment worthy of lesser bus girls: "Gol, that was a fast bath. Wish they could all go that fast."

XI.

The man that marries one of them has done an act of Christian charity which entitles him to the kindly applause of mankind, not their harsh censure—and the man that marries sixty of them has done a deed of openhanded generosity so sublime that the nations should stand uncovered in his presence and worship in silence.

–Mark Twain, *Roughing It*

To get the obvious question out on the table, I propose to ask it outright, which seems only efficient–though, frankly, I had no way of knowing the answer then, and have even less of a notion now that I've plunged into post-mid-life testosterone decline. No thanks to the blind botcher of creation's chore, my mind's not quite half as dirty as it once was. But I hope you'll permit me at least to wonder out loud whether our condiment-encrusted bus chickadees, in their feathery freshness, were tickled to be frog-marched past Augie's buckin' broncos and through the Hell gate. Did they wakefully partake, like that seasoned sex-worker Magdalen, of primordial left-path licentiousness? Or did they just lie back in stretchers and brainlessly submit, like regular Mormon females, to an earthly existence of perpetual fecundation and a birth rate no less subcontinental than the Tantrism that knocks them up and up and up like little white ping pong balls off a horizontal paddle?

It was an abnormally large number of years since most of them had started sloughing surplus uterine lining. This desert being situated down-wind of open-air hydrogen bomb tests that knocked everyone's bio-clocks silly, the children were already high-yield conduits of the magically efficacious *Elixir Rubeus*. That catamenic consideration alone qualified them for the signal honor of participating in *The Mass of the Phoenix*. Thus was overridden any mere adherence to an arbitrary statute enacted by uninitiate secular authority, ignored in any case by a goodly portion of the local populace, Tantric or non-. The give-

and-take upon which practical polygamy is based necessitates a marriageable age of twelve.

Here in this Forty-Fifth State of the Union, prepubescent pinkies can wax connubial, pending receipt of parental permission, of course. And a synonym for *parent* in this familistically convoluted zone is *Patriarch*. You see, Mr. Glasscock is not only Owner-Proprietor of the Telestial Spaw, but also the ringleader of a bunch of lesser Latter Day lechers. Status as "Prophet-Seer-Revelator" is requisite for any self-respecting Alpha polygamist, because lackeys and acolyte-flunkes, by holding down day jobs as Rural Free Delivery mailmen, etc., generate the pooled income necessary for the sustenance of plural espousedness. It's a kind of navel-down communism with a clean-shaven satyriac playing Stalin.

Our chicks were certainly too young and green and juicy for their sex and its dewy fluids to require ritualization. But this is not to say such practices were unknown outside the Telestial Spaw, in other more, shall we say, mainstream zones of *Our Lovely Deseret Where the Saints of Gawd Have Met*. This off-color joke of a political entity was settled, after all, every tree hand-planted, every drop of moisture laboriously duped down from the mountainsides, by followers of men with dozens of wives, hundreds of horny children, and terribly hideous sideburns. Our small civilization wasn't one-three-hundredth as superannuated as the subcontinent's, in many parts of which, according to the Mighty Pythoness of Dnepropetrovsk, the perverted anti-authority of the Tantras long ago tragically superceded the "clean and poetical hymns of the Rig Veda." But the harmonies of those ancient and beautiful hymns were drowned out by panting and grunting here in the Extreme Occident as well. And it wasn't just a belated sexy-sixties thing—though that didn't hurt, or help.

This is beginning to sound like a self-hating hick's diatribe against the toxic turf upon which his dam did him the disservice of dropping him. But you don't need to trek all the way out into my desert to find a place where the clean, poetical Rig Vedic hymns are drowned out by pathology. How about getting spiffed up and going continental with me?

Let's elevate ourselves and our discourse and take a proper jumbo jet to no less a bastion of taste and lawfulness and high old civilization than the glamorous Stauffenberg Castle in scenic Wilflingen. It's the *Deutschland* domicile of a family of thirteenth-century-vintage Imperial Knights, not the least of whom is the would-be Hitler-killer portrayed so poignantly by handsome, talented Tom Cruise in the Hollywood blockbuster.

There, if we behave ourselves and stop mouth-breathing like retarded Salt Flat jackrabbits, we may drop in upon *Herren* Junger *und* Hofmann. The former is reciprocating the latter's earlier invitation, and is hosting a replay of the "first planned psychedelic test."

Once again, Mozart spirals on the phonographic spindle. But which Mozart?

XII.

The Aryan tribe has forded you, River.
Now let your fast streams flow.
I crave your favor who deserve our worship.
                        —Rig Veda, Hymn xxxiii

Dare we hope this time to overhear some proper Mozart for a change? As we take our brain-jaunt to the land of Schopenhauer and Nietzsche, is it too much to ask that we be allowed to eavesdrop on a composition which redounds not with shame but unparalleled glory upon the composer's name? As we stand among the pygmy ponies with Augie the Uncompahgre and try to ignore our underage coworkers' snorts of greasy rut, will we be subjected again to the Flarp-Flop? Or will our blood-brain barrier get the boon of a proper symphony? Dare we aspire to be put in mind of this pertinent passage from the Sage Parashara—

> *...the minds of some who live at the end of Kali Yuga shall be awakened and become as pellucid as crystal.*

If anyone who has languished in this long Age of Impurity ever possessed a mind describable as pellucid and crystalline, it is Mozart. But I'm not talking about the bored hireling who piddled the whimpering climax of my luncheon buffet repertoire. Rather I refer, with hushed reverence, to the Seer-Revelator whose prime prophecy is named after the greatest of gods, who gave the godliest shout between Bach and Beethoven. The symphony I am referring to does the opposite of the flute and harp concerto: brooking few harmonic restraints, out-Baching Bach himself (who exhaled counterpoint like greenhouse gas), it displays crystalline pellucidity of mind unsurpassed in any field of human endeavor, if that's not too ambitious a claim.

Since, in the subcontinental scheduling scheme, we are talking about hardly imaginable expanses of time, and since the present Kali Yuga has lasted, according to one conservative estimate, more than a myriad of years, it's axiomatic that Mozart, like us, lived in the tail-end of the End Time. If a clear demonstration of that miserable datum is needed, consider that he composed this particular symphony for a crass casino, got fucked out of the paltry fee, and wound up never hearing it performed. Nevertheless, solely on the basis of an awestricken scan of the score, the impresario was moved to dub it *Jupiter*, because only the greatest of godly ears could encompass all five voices of the fourth movement's *fugato* finale.

We can assume pellucidity of mind was among the goals Ernst Junger hoped to attain via the agency of Hofmann's new Soma. So, as the acid comes on to our Master Racial entheonauts in the glam Stauffenberg Castle, do you reckon the platter they're spinning is the Symphony No. 41 in C Major? Or is it the Flarp-Fuck after all?

Before you hazard a guess, consider this bit of gossip about a former Great God from beyond the Khyber Pass. In our penultimate age of decay, our gloomy Kali Yuga, when egotism has spread like swinish influenza, Indra, the Hindu Jupiter, is degraded to a sloppy drunkard. But, in the beginning, he was among the doughtiest of the Aryan pantheon. In the Rig Veda his Soma-tripping allegorizes a vigorous, wholesome, pellucid spirituality.

Consider this hint: the Rig Vedic equivalent of the Jupiter Sym-phony—that is to say, the finest of all hymns to the Hindu Jupiter—was not accompanied by an untouchable teen-boy with unmanicured nails scratching ditties from a few dozen offscourings of a dead cat's intestine for the edification of mongrel *mlecchas* who gobbled hanta-viral rodent gristle off unsanitary trenchers. No, indeed, when the Aryans sang the praises of Indra, a pedigreed Brahman was conscripted to ply a plectrum of the rarest rattan upon a harp of a hundred strings dextrously spun from blades of karmically impeccable munga grass. And the only caloric intake was of Soma, in a recipe that called for clarified (which is to say *pellucid*) butter.

What about the recipe for the second "planned psychedelic test"? Was it well-planned as the first? Ernie, who throughout his shrapnel- and bullet-riddled WWI glory days was a big ether and cocaine man, added an ingredient that will not surprise the alert reader with its essential militarism. This old death-worshiping Iron Cross honoree, all jagged and speedy, is every bit as much of a stock character in the rollicking Kali Yuga skit as my spermo-gnostic boss and his quasi-Kabbalistic jailbait. Who better to stride through the Age of Destruction than Destruction Personified, the Soldier? And here's the uncannily contemporary-sounding reason Herr *Mut und Tod und Blut und Boden* gives for stirring in more than a soupçon of speed:

> *I perceive in our time less of a taste for the* phantastica *than for the* energetica. *Amphetamine, which has even been furnished to fliers and other soldiers by the armies, belongs to this group.*

Now I'll give you one more chance to predict this soiree's musical menu–but only after you've heard some of the prose conceived that day in the Stauffenberg Castle–

> *Now a breath of air affected the vision, and softly twisted it about the shaft like a dancer. He uttered a shout of surprise. The beams and lattices of the wondrous flower wheeled around in new planes, in new fields. Myriads of molecules observed the harmony. Here the laws no longer acted under the veil of appearance; matter was so delicate and weightless that it clearly reflected them. How simple and cogent everything was. The numbers, masses and weights stood out from matter. They cast off the raiments.*

Having read that, go ahead and tell me which piece of vinyl was impaled on the gramophone. But keep in mind these lines from the Sage Parashara, regarding the select few at the end of the Kali Yuga, whose minds will become "pellucid as crystal"–

> *The men who are thus changed...shall be the seeds of human beings, and shall give birth to a race who shall follow the laws of...the Age of Purity.*

Evidently, if that text is to be believed, Mozart's dharma was to sire a new race (of which your narrator must be a mutant abortion–hence the dead foetal cover imagery of this flip book, with its strangling tangle of umbilical bowel). It follows, contrariwise, that, despite his Aryan affectations, the function of Junger, and also of that other stock character in the Kali Yugic skit, Albert Hofmann–dissolver of so many young brains in the late sixties and early seventies (as you may have noticed)–was to hasten the general decline and make room for the Mozartean spawn. Ergo, Mozart is a Vedic artist, Junger a post-Vedic. Psychedelic writing is the current degenerate Indra, pissy drunk, while Mozart is the earlier god, stoned on proper Soma, before the identity of the key ingredient in the lovely milky recipes was forgotten.

The former Indra and his avatars are the proper auditors for the Symphony No. 41 in C Major. So, you were incorrect if that was your answer. Junger's speedy adulterant explains the *Flöte- und Harfekonzert*'s presence on the program this time as well. They gave that sad spewing of crap a rerun, eschewing the Jupiter, and not just because of the gentile personnel listed in the album notes. The Flarp-Flop turns out to be the sort of unkosher decoration with which fascists prefer to bespangle their puffy chests.

Picture this avatar of destruction, pleased with his warlike self, his own Genghis Khannishness, his Mannishness-in-Time (to use Savitri Devi's terms), his brain-vagina pried open for the first time with history's freshest batch of LSD. What if he gets suddenly wounded in all his post-Prussian peacock vanity by music which even the Nazis regarded with "mistrust and fear"? Who knows how a man injured umpteen times in WWI and given up for dead at least once, yet ornery enough to live more than a hundred years, would react to such a bum trip? Doilies could fly in that hoity-toity castle. Better stick to the ear tinsel.

So, it turns out there was only one choice of tunes possible. Can you imagine what would have happened if Hofmann, in his quality as deejay for the day, had been courageous enough to spin a Jew platter? I doubt Junger would have written any brittle bits of relic *Romantik*, or anything else, for that matter. He would have been flat and unmilitaristically on his ass, on the floor, maybe clinging like a cockroach to the ceiling, questioning his own place in the universal muster, and realizing the mere Kali Yugic functionality of his beloved war.

If he wrote anything at all, it would have been long after the acid wore off, and it might have been astonishing. Note this passage which closes the paragraph:

> *The pyramids with their weight did not reach up to this revelation. That was Pythagorean luster. No spectacle had ever affected him with such a magic spell. No goddess could inform the initiates more boldly and freely.*

Junger's final denial is an affirmation. Hofmann, who shooed away his *Hausfrau* after she'd fetched the cocoa, certainly never imagined, in neither a positive or negative way, till his interlocutor broached it, the possibility of such a female presence hovering in the background, ever-present, sharing a shivering common spine, *softly turning about the shaft like a dancer,* inverted like a female crucifee, like Mrs. Glasscock-Five, the Shakti Avatar Kali, like the beautiful bus girl with the flaring nostrils.

But what of sweet old Albert? The alert reader will be no less surprised to hear that, as a result of the speed, Hofmann got fucked with the famous "horror trip," history's first bummer, which couldn't have been less cleanly, poetical or Rig Vedic. Junger's crank gave birth to LSD's daddy's Regan, his Goneril, his Woodstock Brown.

I have little doubt the gentle Swiss chemist, drowning in the double bummer of high potency uppers and abysmal-quality Mozart, found his astral self transtemporally plopped in the Telestial Spaw's Private Bath, smack in the dead center of the conjure circle, surrounded by hideous, naked, stretch-marked, semen-, menses- and excrement-smeared specimens of the screwy broads he would never have allowed on one of his own pristine Platonic trips. Everything has changed for the worse, especially the music, which has puckered, courtesy of your narrator, into an embarrassment of its already shameful self. Meanwhile Jimmy Page halitoticizes down Al's neck. Bummer is not the word.

I wonder what unforgettable depths of blood Hofmann saw in his interlocutor's eyes that stoned day in the Stauffenberg Castle. When the reporter from the New York Whatever showed up on his hundredth birthday and asked him if his "problem child" had brought him any insights into death, the poor son of a bitch, even at that late date, jumped back in startlement and had nothing to offer in reply. The militaristic amphetamine still scoured those resilient old arteries long after the LSD had settled impotently in his body fat.

XIII.

Our hope lies in young people who suffer from fever because they eat the green pus of disgust.
　　　　　　　　　　　　–Ernst Junger,
　　　　　　　　　　　　Das abenteuerliche Herz

"Well, well, well," I remark aptly to my redskin pal. "Jimmy Page himself is beneath my feet at this very moment, eh? Don't tell me: he's the one with the squeaky voice in the sopranino register, like a lady sperm whale advertizing estrus through a vay-jay in the tippity-top of her head, as follows:

> *There's a world where I can go*
> *and tell my secrets to*
> *In my roooooom, in my roooooom*
> *In this world I lock out all my*
> *worries and my fears*
> *In my roooooom, in my roooooom*
>
> *Do my dreaming and my scheming*
> *Lie awake and pra-a-a-a-a-ay*
> *Do my crying and my sighing*
> *Laugh at yesterda-a-a-a-ay...*"

I apologize to my readers for shrieking like that. I'm just trying to drown out the orgasm grunts, both postmenopausal and prepubescent, that echo from the Private Bath. And there's an even more egregious layer of sonic feces to contend with. A mid-sized mob of Bitch Boy fans have caught wind of our illustrious guest's presence, and have seeped up from the city. They're gathered in the salt and tar and sulphur at the Telestial Spaw gate. The pertinent moron pulsations blast from their shoulder-deployed ghetto blasters.

Suddenly comes a gross bestial response to this mating call. Geysering like geothermal mush up from the pores in the travertine and into every corner of this horsey barracks, it's a loud, hideous, single rock 'n roll chord, an unextended dominant seventh in the first inversion, pounded over and over. The bass has been turned all the way up on the six-inch speakers strapped to our RFD mailman's pelvis: undirected aggression, whipped to a froth and made audible for dead brains, to jostle the skull-blood and simulate a living pulse.

Evidently, at this point on the audio tape, the house harpist has unwedged the tool of his trade from between his labia majora and wandered off for one of his increasingly extended breaks. As usual, in the name of Rapid High-Volume Patron Turnover, the boss has caused the radio to blare over the sound system, to occupy customers' ears while I'm out here philosophizing and psychedelicizing with Augie the Uncompahgre.

Inspired by Mr. Page's descent upon this misspelled heck-hole, Glasscock has decided to put top-ten Hit Parade pop-rock on the PA instead of 50,000-watt clear-channel KSL Radio News. The patrons get no reports of grisly murders to digest by, just grisly music, the sort of torture originally intended to be administered through three-inch dashboard speakers, the undifferentiated Wall of Sound plastered across America by what's-his-name, the future wife-killer.

In my junior year of high school, it's just starting to be allowed on the Frequency Modulation bandwidth, theretofore reserved for classical stations, which were thought to require and deserve the superior sound quality. It would only be a few more years before the classics would pucker up like cold scrota and shrivel off the AM band to which they were banished. Jazz, of course, the whole time, during both eras, could be heard on neither. Jimmy Page should've been born an autistic bonobo. At least he wouldn't go mad with monotony like the rest of us forced to live in a world saturated with his idiocy.

The limitations shackling a top-ten Hit Parade rock-popper are more severe, but similar in kind to those self-imposed by the composer and performer of the Flarpathon. A pop-rock outfit's bassist is chained like a retarded harpist's feet to the dungeon floor, only able to writhe a bit over two or three notes, obsessive-compulsive as a dumb beast who can't keep from gnawing an open sore on a forelimb. This contrasts with the bass lines of, say, for example, the Jupiter Symphony (which my Spaw fans would never be able to sit through—it would make them nervous, irritate their bowels, no doubt). Down there on the bottom, Mozart's celli, doubled by his contrabassi, remain free as angel armies of either polarity to fly upon the aether.

Angels of the light appeal less than dungeons and chains to the warlock who signs my under-the-table paychecks. Glassy Cock considers himself, and is considered by others, to be Aleister Crowley *redivivus*. So, in his establishment where the Flarpathon is featured upstairs, why would anyone be surprised to hear that Jimmy Page has materialized downstairs?

Mel Torme called it "three-chord manure," this idiocy they've been hammering into our heads ever since Alan "Moondog" Freed wiped his ass on Cleveland's airwaves sixty years ago: the fascist noise which simultaneously anaesthetizes and tortures us in every restaurant, elevator, gas station, glory hole, mega-church, and cretinous movie soundtrack; the rock-'n-retch which Homeland Security's mercenaries employed to turn Jose Padilla into an end table.

Make no mistake, they plan to Padilla all our asses. Heaven forefend we should have a quiet minute to think and maybe even talk politics. Why do you suppose the Trans-National Corporatocracy maintains pet execs in the recording industry? Howcome do you reckon they soak everybody's existence, in-utero onward, with perpetual grunting decibels? Do you think it's coincidental that our gallant troops ipod this sonic dreck into the sides of their learning-disabled heads while marauding through the scab-clogged gutters of Ur of the Chaldees?

You don't hear much ambient jazz these days, do you? Betty Carter singing "Moonlight in Vermont"–could she persuade you to shoot an Ishmaelite baby in the back? Eric Dolphy sipping "Epistrophe" from the silver bell of his bass clarinet– does he make you want to kick down a door and rape a veiled grandmother? Bill Harris sliding a bright "Bijou" from his trombone, Clifford Brown letting "Joy Spring" from his young trumpet, Bix Beiderbecke sweetly floating "In a Mist"–do they put you in the mood to hover in a helicopter and shit brimstone that melts the skin off schoolchildren's bones in Gaza?

One day people will look back at the Dark Age that began with the second half of the twentieth century, and they will recognize this screaming, pounding, migrainous aural-expulsiveness as a symptom of humanity's contemptible degeneration, right along with mega-meat farms, television, Ritalin, the collected works of Mark Helprin, the military application of that substance which sizzles between silicon and sulfur on the Periodic Table of Elements, and the cold-blooded politicide of the Palestinian people.

The militaristic fascist lockstep of rock is ideal for pumping into the dupes whom the Power Structure wants numb and posthypnotically suggestible. Do you really think it's the "music" that sells all those trillions of records? Where's the pleasure in having your eardrums traumatized by a grown man shrieking like an unhappy prepubescent girl? Junger lived long enough to have his regimental heart warmed by this post-Vedic noise.

The *Flöte- und Harfekonzert* notwithstanding, Mozart's soul was hearty even while his body was fixing to be dumped in a mass grave full of other anonymous paupers. On the other hand, multi-millionaire top-ten Hit Parade pop-rockers hobble arthritically across the earth's surface today who are twenty-five, thirty, thirty-five years older than the age Mozart maxed out at, whose souls were already putrid and decayed fifteen years before that, whose vocal cords continue taking a murderous toll on the airwaves.

XIV.

Come writers and critics
Who prophesize [sic] *with your pen...*
—top-ten Hit Parade
pop-rock song

Ernst Junger, when nine years old, began to read the *Arabian Nights*, which he would come to call "this immortal gift of the magical world to the West." Note the M-word. Stare at it long enough with the gritty eyeballs of a teen-boy on phosphorescent green goat blotter acid, and you will see a lower-case "k" materialize among its seven letters. What could be the reason for this?

Synchronism is the reason. On the same night, at the very moment when jailbait Junger curled up with Scheherazade, not only did the embryonic Father of LSD curl up on Frau Hofmann's uterine wall, but the future Wickedest Man in the World curled up in the King's Chamber of the Great Pyramid at Gizeh and got fecundated with supernal wisdom by a falcon-headed god. That very same epochal year Crowley wrote the notoriously cryptic *Sword of Song, Called by Early Christians the Book of the Beast*. Among its infinite convolutions and meta-para-volutions, this book contains a twenty-seven-word tercet (I'll share it with you presently) that was to have the effect on my life of a K-turn executed at speed by a Bradley Urban Assault Vehicle.

On that busy night so long ago, inside the big dusty simplistic building in the Cairo suburbs, Divine Horus graced Crowley with a revelation that would result in the institution of the Thelemic cult and its vast library of revealed scripture, such as *The Mass of the Phoenix, White Stains* and numerous other *magickal* writings. These have proven seductive to transgressive bibliophiles like Mr. Glasscock, and to one other collector very unlike my boss.

"Augie, hold on a sec. Did you say Jimmy Page is down there trying to—"

"Buy something. Yeah."

Like so many disaffected youngsters in that remote era of the Kali Yuga, I had several of the Horus-inspired Thelemic texts by heart, and some proto-Thelemic texts as well, both canonical and apocryphal, especially *Sword of Song, Called by Early Christians the Book of the Beast.* That one in particular, chief among all the others, was collated among my head's axons and dendrites, strophe for non-strophe, neologism for paleologism. It tended to flutter when one kinky entheogenic substance or other was infiltrating the opaque matter between my brain's synaptic clefts.

I could always tell when some acid was kicking in, because *Sword of Song, etc.*'s beastly pages began to appear pasted like handbills upon whatever walls happened to surround me, or not, at the moment. We disaffected youngsters ruffled the leaves of this liturgy in our minds, deriving cryptic prophecies to guide the day, as pagans used to do with the *Aeneid*, while our lesser schoolmates were staring slack-jawed at Crowley's visage, taken in vain on the cover of a long-playing phonograph record lately pressed by their favorite top-ten Hit Parade pop-rock outfit, Herman and the Hermits, or whoever.

"The Monkees," says Augie.

"Oh, yeah. That's right."

Speaking of The Monkees, Jimmy Page is on tour with his top-ten Hit Parade pop-rock outfit. Like a subcontinental king who has sacrificed the white horse and become a full-blown Chakravarti, he has entered upon the intra-monsoon campaign season, and is dragging his entire moving city across the green plushness of the Hindustan: retainers, flunkies, body guards, vulnerable baggage boys, harem fodder, eunuch wife protectors, camp followers, foragers, scouts, camel and elephant wranglers; not to mention techies, groupies, admen, media managers, booking agents, roadies, spin-off merch hawkers, engineers for the mixing board, specialists to tweak the pop-rock instruments and lug shit around, sundry other roadies for lights, construction, advance-men, drivers, pyrotechnicians, legal team, wardrobe, catering support crew, sundry random butt boys, and some weird little yogins skittering about in the marginal weeds. (I believe it's from their eye sockets the phosphorescent chartreuse goat acid is wept.) The proverbial Hindu autocrat is on progress, and Maharaja Jimmy has decreed a detour from the emerald Punjab into our squalid Thar Desert, for what reason nobody outside the Private Bath, and your narrator, can imagine.

And how could those trans-Khyber types, both Aryan and mleccha, know such a king was coming? Why, by the sound of his mountain-sized drum, which was carried on the backs of six straining bull elephants and beaten with a two-thousand-year-old banyan tree trunk strung on a sky-high series of block-and-tackle engines, the gargantuan cleverness of which would have put the Romans to shame as they besieged Jerusalem. A quite large percussion instrument it was, indeed, and it could be heard from a fair ways off.

And I hear a distant drum this evening in the Telestial Spaw Righteous Wrangler Riding Stable. As the last cellulose fiber of the blotter succumbs to my saliva (which, unlike a termite's, was never intended to digest such stuff), a distant drum-riff occurs to my memory, from *Sword of Song, Called by Early Christians the Book of the Beast*—

> *To aid the hotch-potch, lyre and lute*
> *replace by liar and loot; the harp and flute*
> *make dumb; the drum doth come and make us mute...*

From an even greater distance—the space between dendrites in my skull—I hear Baphomet's pounding line, pound again.

It gives me pause with all the whip-lash of a balking pony, astonishing me to a scalp-corrugating degree–

The drum doth come and make us mute.

It's all clear now, right? The harp, the flute? The drum? I hear a dumb-making drum, and it's coming, thumping, the herald and harbinger of Jimmy Page, who just happens to be the world's most anally retentive collector of Crowleyana. Old books soaking up geothermal steam in the Private Bath are the *loot*. Glasscock is the *liar*.

My spine snaps like a towel in a bathroom when I realize how eerily exact the prophecy has turned out, all these years and miles away from the circumstances in which it was revealed to that tosser and turner on gritty sarcophagi, that Horus fornicator, in the King's Chamber–

The harp and flute make dumb.

The rock star has dragged his moveable population center to our Spaw solely to enhance his collection of Crowley relics. He is soliciting from Glassy Cock an item which has come into the latter's hands by a route better left untraced (a certain gargantuan museum in London was burgled: enough said).

The desideratum is one of those scriptures composed by, rather, divinely dictated to Baphomet himself. The Wickedest Man in the Word dug into the flesh of his birthright and drained his own spirit's menstrual blood to quicken and infuse this poetry. Crowley's literary vocation was itself the *Elixir Rubeus*, and he put himself into bankruptcy in order to bind his writings in the most beautiful and costly leather. But, in his innocence of base retail behavior, he allowed some filthy member of the merchant caste, a slinger of inferior textiles, to sell him a most ephemeral sort of thread with which to stitch his sublime vanity books.

As a result, the volumes are crumbling to the touch by the time the perfectly named Mr. Page descends into the black Glasscockian Cathedral-*inversus*. The books sold under my feet are in plastic bags, already three-fourths dust, a mere few dozen years after the Beast caused them to be placed, for posterity, in the British Museum.

Hear now Crowley's truest utterance, truer even than the lyrics to his *Mass of the Phoenix*–

> *...my responsibility to the gods was to write as I was inspired; my responsibility to mankind was to publish what I wrote. But it ended there. As long as what I wrote was technically accessible to the public...my hands were clean.*

Those approximately three dozen words, taken from the Great Beast 666's *Autohagiography*, morally encapsulate the existence I happen to be mired in. So let me lay them on you again–

> *...my responsibility to the gods was to write as I was inspired; my responsibility to mankind was to publish what I wrote. But it ended there. As long as what I wrote was technically accessible to the public...my hands were clean.*

This both breaks and bolsters my heart every time I read it. Three repeats make a conjure formula. One more once, as Count Basie used to say–

> *...my responsibility to the gods was to write as I was inspired; my responsibility to mankind was to publish what I wrote. But it ended there. As long as what I wrote was technically accessible to the public...my hands were clean.*

Sounds like just the thing to be handled by a rock-whore's lucre-smutched paws, for a private collector privately to collect, and to hoarde.

A certain high school junior you have come know and love received his life's vocation at that moment. *The harp and flute make dumb*, indeed. I saw the irony of my position as clearly as Crowley's. And, in a flash of associations, as they say, I understood that, all along, even as early as the year I shoved the harp up my birth canal, it wasn't the sounds, not what oozed from the vinyl grooves, but the words, the bits of typography glowing from the album notes, that spoke properly to my ear.

XV.

Anterior to all the stages of his life which brought him fame, however, was the period when he was Joyce the [musician].... *All he wanted was a lute made by Dolmetch* [sic]...

–Oliver St. John Gogarty

By this point, if you haven't already dumped me head first and flipped me aside in favor of Deb Hoag, your mind will have responded to the subtle hints and come to the conclusion that, in his penultimate year of high school, and, no doubt, ever thereafter, your narrator had no business masquerading as a votary of Euterpe. You'll have decided he is no born musician. He won't even be a dead one when the time comes. Our provisionally named narrator, Tom Bradley, turns out to be a born and eventually-to-be-dead something else altogether. What might that be?

The musicking was just a salad-day scam, dreamt up in the presence of folks for whom a salad consists of three limp iceberg lettuce leaves smothered under Crisco-fried croutons and sexual globs of trans-fatty ranch-style dressing. The indifferent pickers at such salads were prediabetically stuporous enough to ignore me three afternoons and evenings a week as I tarted up like Wayne Newton and barely pretended to earn just enough untaxed under-the-table dough to lie low, idle and acid-addled the rest of the time.

Never mind the beautiful bus girl with the flaring nostrils. I seduced these malnourished Latter Day slobs into the Secret Sex Pot of my moral sloth. I had no business doing that–unless the idle time was spent emptying my head, draining it, till the inside of my skull became a featureless desert where I could stumble about like Jesus and listen to the demons, monsters and Hairy Ones cry out, and tell them to get behind me, or in front, as the case might be.

What other lifetime career besides musicking among lumpen-hicks entails so much temporal and mental liberty—actually, a bit more?

Little though I suspected at the time, each of my shifts at the Telestial Spaw, along with its hourly forty-five minute break, prepared me for my current blissful, slothful death-in-life, way over here on the opposite side of the planet. The sordid Flarpathonic gig about which you've been reading was regular vocational training for your narrator. (Italicize that last word if you need a hint as to what he currently "does," so to speak.)

Once you've attained the point in life where you can look backwards and put an "s" at the end of the word "decade" without descending into pubeless baby-talk, you've accumulated a span of years sufficient to survey and conclude, "This is karma." You've already begun to learn dispassion and disinterest, and to achieve that "pellucidity as of crystal" which the Sage Parashara promised to certain minds in the End Times.

No need to carry a biochipped Hindu Sympathizer card and get all vulgar and specific about "past lives." Just try this notion as a general working hypothesis, a mental exercise, for the sake of argument: your vitality extends beyond a single paltry existence. Not you per se, but the essential existent underlying and motivating you has more than one crack at getting this so-called "being" rigmarole right.

Something interesting happens when you employ hindsight thus focused. Every moment in the past becomes metaphorical for every other, a precis, or post-cis. A happily amoral sense is made of your time in this particular coat of skin. Those years of youth an occidental mind dismisses as "misspent" now transcend the preterite, subsuming tense itself. Those "wild oats" that you previously considered "sown" bounce back into the seed bag. You can perform a kind of auto-Midrash, such as our Hebraic pals do with their tribal autobiography, only microcosmically. And you find that you've been constantly reincarnating inside your head ever since the moment it breached your mom's sticky placenta.

Some people are born in conditions of waterless sub-Saharan penury or AIDS babyhood. Others grow up in occupied territories, multinational corporocratic mercenaries asperging them with white phosphorus as they toddle to kindergarten. My karma, on the other hand, is to be put on display for tiny amounts of time per week in front of small numbers of uncomprehending, indifferent, utterly alien souls. This was the moral essence of my livelihood as a teen, and it's exactly the same now. Yet another hint: in both instances I am flat on my ass and in my stocking feet.

Here is one significant difference among many: in the earlier case I was not free to drink proper coffee, only tepid saucers of Sanka decaf, while in my current incarnation I am considered eccentric for swilling only a couple liters of green tea each day. It's under the latter leaf-rich, as opposed to the former bean-poor conditions, that I have found my art.

What art would flourish fueled by the one but not the other? Let's consult our old psychoactive expert, Ernst Junger, one last time. Hear him weighing in on those two verboten hot drinks:

> *Tea is in my opinion a phantasticum, coffee an energeticum. Tea therefore possesses a disproportionately higher artistic rank. I notice that coffee disrupts the delicate lattice of light and shadows, the fruitful doubts that emerge during the writing of a sentence. One exceeds his inhibitions. With tea, on the other hand, the thoughts climb genuinely upward.*

So, where can you get a do-nothing, sit-down, stocking-feet job, and meanwhile be steeped in the brew which conduces to the writing of sentences?

Here's another geo-dietary hint: *panem nostrum quotidianum*-wise, where can you go, if not precisely to *earn* so much as to *steal* your *daily*, if not exactly bread, then your gummy wads of swamp cereal, scrubbed of nearly all nutritional value, croutons without the Crisco?

Ever since I was old enough to understand the connections among time and money and eating, I knew I'd eventually have to starve, or become a different person (a karmic non sequitur, of course), or else wind up feigning work in a place like the Telestial Spaw, where the folk might as well have been born without auditory nerves. As soon as I was able to grasp how long an hour is, and to string eight of them together in my imagination, it struck me as preposterous and grotesque that such an infinitude of riches should be squandered five times a week merely in order to postpone the flesh's inevitable slippage from the spirit.

Before I was old enough to be aware that other countries, languages and races exist, I knew everything worth knowing about the nihilistic sham called Japanese academe, and the sinecures it offers to pedagogical sociopaths like me. Hence the eventual necessity of showing America my long, skinny white ass and relocating to this ludicrous side of the International Date Line. Like Joyce laying aside the Dolmetch *[sic]* dream-lute and indenturing himself at the Trieste Berlitz storefront, I junked my Lyon & Healy clunker and became an expatriate schoolmarm.

The essentials of my duties at the Telestial Spaw Pioneer-Style Steam Buffet (and by "essentials," obviously, I don't mean anything musical) could have been choreographed in a time chamber, considering the uncanny parallels with my present gig.

In both the extreme oriental and far western milieux, with nil numbers of words coming from the front of my face, I doze in front of an un-Englished audience, who stare at me with equal amounts of incomprehension. I pretend to ply them with ideas foreign to their ears. The Mormons were no better prepared to hear Mozart than the Nippo-kids are to hear the difference between the R and L in *Bradley*.

As a harpist, I hadn't missed my calling altogether, but merely dealt it a glancing blow. My vocational peg was, indeed, karmically determined to find its hole onstage. I saunter into the Nippo-classroom and mount a dais designed to aid dwarf-sized colleagues in their efforts to reach a chalkboard that's flush with my belly button.

I flop down in the professorial comfy chair, put my stocking feet up on the professorial lectern, fart, adjust my balls and relax. I lay my manuscript in the lap that once received a harp, and, loosely, easefully, with my medium-point Bic, begin to dig down till I get all the way back home, through the salt and tar to the travertine base of my skull.

The rest is silence. You'll be gratified to know that this very morning, Nanjing Rapists' grandchildren paid twice Harvard's tuition rate to sit and silently watch me scribble this stuff. Since it's impossible to keep a straight face and simultaneously pretend that an actual higher-educational environment can exist in a Confucian culture, I don't bother to order my captive audience to pull their pencils from their Hello Kitty satchels.

In fact, I forgot their existence altogether as I wrote the impishly endearing depiction of myself trying and failing to befriend that beautiful bus girl with the flaring nostrils. I neglected to excuse the unhappy zits at the end of class because I was so engrossed in removing a comma which I'd placed under the watchful eyes of their schoolmates during the previous period. By the time Augie so ill-advisedly let slip the name of Led Zeppelin's resident dilettante Crowleyite, the Pavlovian lunch bell had rung. But not so much as a single salivary gland stirred, for our Nipponese brethren do nothing, not even secrete, without permission from a superior authority.

As you and I segued ever so naturally into my rollicking yet poignant anecdote about history's "first planned psychedelic test," the sound of a few polite throat-clearings was heard from among the midget-sized desks ranged so neatly in front of me. The poor swindled youngsters tried to penetrate my museful haze, for they hankered to scurry on bandy legs to the varsity cafeteria and nibble their gummy wads of colonically cancerous swamp cereal, their dioxin-drenched sperm whale burgers, and their bottlenose dolphin tacos with extra mercury. Gradually, as the lunch period wasted further and further away, my disciples escalated to coughs outright. This is what passes for student rebellion, here in the World's Safest Country.

Eventually the place starts to sound like a phosphorus-bombed consumptive's clinic in post-apocalyptic Gaza. But even this can't recall to your faithful narrator's mind the location of his body.

In the meantime, if he happens to cause a few words to be juxtaposed happily, Tom Bradley might look up, grin graciously at his adoring public, and shout a hearty "Bravo!" to himself: "...*top-ten Hit Parade pop-rock outfit*–well put, Doctor Bradley, well put!"

There are clear parallels between the Duke of Guînes, Adrien-Louis de Bonnières' daughter and my pupils. But the divergences are more telling: poor Mozart had at least to pretend he was in the same room as the nibbling, grasping vampire of his vitality. He couldn't sit back and compose the Jupiter Symphony. I, on the other hand, wrote this half of our flip book while ignoring the presence of inferior beings, except perhaps to recite an especially delicious passage to the unpopular nerd who twitches solitarily in the front row of every classroom on either side of the Pacific.

No matter how many lunches he misses, this one little ass-kisser will sit up straight and keep his bespectacled eyes nailed on the Master, ready to provide whatever audience response his idol requires in this "loneliest of labors," including moans and tears and gnashings of teeth in those rare instances when the word juxtaposition turns out not so happy. Scratch-outs are occasionally called for, accompanied by the bellowing of mild self-critical strictures: "...*my long, skinny white ass*–that could have been better put, don't you think, Doctor Bradley?" Who says the writerly craft's a solitary one? Not me. I am gregarious as Wayne Newton at his most exhibitionistic.

If you are petit-bourgeois, the phrase *job security* will have popped into your head. But put your mind at ease. This scribbling outlander's beard, skin and eyes–red white and blue respectively–have dazzled the gibberish-belching university administrators into taking his unconscionable goldbricking for an advanced application of the latest Language Acquisition Theory developed in the laboratories of Big Name U., America. Therefore it must be an excellent investment in their proud nation's future. He has even given his crime of omission a name that croons unrivaled trendiness: "You guys have heard of distance learning, right? Well, this is distance teaching." The signers of his paychecks are persuaded to turn a deaf ear to any appalled complaints from mere tuition payers.

Think of the gall, the sheer lack of basic potty-trained humanity! The best years of the youngsters' lives are pissing away, right at his feet, and he doesn't just sit there doing nothing (many a mortal schoolmarm manages to accomplish that feat), but he is able, with all these little faces staring at him in indignation and unmitigated hate, to concentrate on the exacting production of archangelically tumescent prose!

How does this sleazy, hairy-armed, big-nosed, good for nothing, barbarous anti-*sensei* do it? Can it be that, as a completely self-centered being, he possesses the most extraordinary powers of concentration, and can deploy his three-dollar words into five-dollar sentences even as his disciples pass out from hunger, one by one? Is it because only a true genius has the cheek to compose when he's the cynosure of rows and rows of malnourished eyes?

If, like me, you are a writer as well as a reader, and if you should ever arrive at a state of affairs where breadwinning leaves you inadequate leisure to compose, please accept my invitation to come here, to the land of cherry blossoms, bukkake, suicide clubs, grown women with baby mouse voices, eight-fingered

Yakuza goons whose tobacco and methedrine reek make you swoon in a typhoon, and the world's greatest tertiary education system, outside Brazil. (I hear profs don't even have to show up there—but you'd better double check that factoid by referring to the great *São Paulo Blues*, by Jim Chaffee.)

Sometimes as I feign pedagogy, I get so relaxed that the manuscript slips from my lap. My brain slips back in time, and I feel as though I've returned to my acid-addled teen-boyishness, dozing through some Andantino or other at the Spaw.

Suddenly, from out of nowhere, an oaken portal marked—

PRIVATE BATH
BY RESERVATION ONLY

—appears and squeaks wide, belching yellow geothermal smoke laced with human fat. My old boss steps forth. He's risen from harrowing Hell, just like Christ, just like me, if Japan can be considered Hell.

Like Ernie and Al, those other self-medicators with the Concerto for Flute, Harp and Orchestra in C Major, KV 299, the Glassy Cock must be over a hundred years old—no thanks to any particular adherence to the health legislation of the *Doctrine and Covenants*.

"I need a Winston," he mutters to an Indian standing next to me.

"Coming up for air, Prophet?" remarks Augie, who seems to have grown some wrinkles and shed some teeth.

"It's either escape or suffocate," replies geezer Glasscock. "That Page creature's breath would gag Beelzebub. Talk about decay of the astral shell. He's got quite a Devachanic probation ahead of him, sad wretch. His brain's too heroin-damaged to distinguish a first printing from a mid-quality photographic facsimile. Thanks to you, Stable Master, for consenting to let your stately Lipizzaner stallions age the binding a bit with their mighty hooves."

Mr. Glasscock glances at his house harpist with an almost infini-tesimal spark of interest. And then, for his own benefit more than ours, as if lecturing a retarded bus girl, this magnificent swindler of Led Zeppelin's lead guitarist proceeds to demonstrate why he is cock of this walk, rock of this glass house, and still my boss.

"This Japan stuff you're spewing is bullshit, Bradley."

"Huh?"

"You didn't go all Oriental to avoid squandering Time's infinite riches on the postponement of your flesh's slippage from your spirit."

"I didn't?"

"No. And you haven't moved to the opposite side of the planet from everybody normal just to scribble."

"I haven't?"

"You are not nearly as far-removed from musicking for Mormons as you preen yourself on being. You remain a teeny-bopper in my employ. Sad wretch."

Mr. Glasscock's face starts to glow a raw hamburger shade of red, in a way that I suppose would be scary to someone who gave a fuck.

"To retain your deviated sense of self-respect, Tom, you may have told anybody who'll listen, such as Augie, that you are using children of the Mikado and their hard-working parents as cash cows while you compose. But I can tell you that no writer puts himself in such a situation for so many decades without a better, or at least more complicated, reason than money.

"Think of the impression you've made on that unpopular bespectacled nerd in the front row. The admiration you have elicited from his racially self-hating postpubescent heart is no doubt the result of semi-conscious acts on your part: flourishes you make with that medium-point Bic under his gaze, which you'd never do alone at night in your Nippo-hovel—unless you really did suck on as many blotters as you claim and are now insane. You are dancing and your pet nerd is applauding. With the educator's eye you'll never own up to possessing, you have seen something in him beyond the lust for a passing grade that narrows his classmates' eyes. You are playing Wayne Newton solos for him. You're selling this terminally un-Englished nerd your books. You are where you are because you want an audience.

"Anyone who's been exiled, like Crowley, and experienced the excruciating isolation of literary effort will see the plausibility of my analysis of your life's motivations, Bradley. To undergo the act of composition in the presence of an audience–a captive audience obliged to remain silent, constrained not to hiss or shuffle their feet or to distract your concentration, yet to console and beguile the loneliness of that lofty crag–"

"Lofty crag? Can I quote you, boss?"

I told you he was no native. Centenarian Glasscock might have a point. I'm forced to concede. Yes, the parallels between Hirohito Hell and the Telestial Spaw are apt, and they extend even to the necromancy. The karmic Midrash meshes like gnashed teeth.

I am the Far Eastern Mr. Glasscock, the celebrant, fasting by the proxy of my students, sacrificing to, conjuring in the name of, evoking a raucous, delightful, orgiastic succubus whose narthex is the mind. She's flipped upside-down and is hovering forever behind me.

I have fetched the Kali Yuga to the archipelago of Hiroshima and Nagasaki. I write in the same way the Glassy Cock contra-Eucharized, with a quasi-Kabbalistic cry of *daemon est deus inversus*. This makes the tape of me butchering Mozart correspond to my half of our flip book. And that makes you, the purchaser, equivalent to those spermatophagous left-path pedophile polygamists.

Or might Indra be invoked rather than Kali? If so (and it is to be hoped), the only question is whether my Hindu Jupiter is the early ecstatic or the late lush. In either case, at his leisure, your narrator is learning how his hands, these erstwhile defilers of Mozart, might be made clean as Crowley's.

When Tom Bradley was a little boy he was given a gazetteer for Christmas. As little boys will, he looked up all the places in the world that start with the F-word. There were two, Fukien in China and Fukuoka in Japan. Little did he suspect that he would one day be exiled to both.

Tom is a former lounge harpist. During his pre-exilic period, he played his own transcriptions of Bach and Debussyin a Salt Lake City synagogue that had been transformed intoa pricey watering hole by a nephew of the Shah of Iran.

He taught British and American literature to Chinese graduate students in the years leading up to the Tiananmen Square massacre. He was politely invited to leave China after burning a batch of student essays about the democracy movement rather than surrendering them to "the leaders."

He wound up teaching conversational skills to freshman dentistry majors in the Japanese "imperial university" where they used to vivisect our bomber pilots and serve their livers raw at festive banquets. But his writing somehow sustains him.

You can read more about him at www.TomBradley.org.

9 780990 760474